CAJUN COOKING

CAJUN COOKING

Norma MacMillan

GALLERY BOOKS
An imprint of W.H. Smith Publishers Inc.
112 Madison Avenue
New York, New York 10016

Published by Gallery Books
A Division of W H Smith Publishers Inc.
112 Madison Avenue
New York, New York 10016

Produced by
Brompton Books Corp.
15 Sherwood Place
Greenwich, CT 06830

ISBN 0-8317-1145-0

Printed in Hong Kong

3 4 5 6 7 8 9 10

The publisher would like to thank the
following for providing some of the props
which are used in the photographs:

David Mellor
4 Sloane Square
London SW1 8EE

David Mellor
26 St James St
Covent Garden
London WC2E 8PA

David Mellor
66 King Street
Manchester M2 4NP

Photography by Clint Brown
Designed by Richard Garratt
Food prepared for photography by
   Ann Page-Wood
Styling by Andrea Brown

Page 1: *Gumbo Z' Herbes (page 9).*
Pages 2-3: *Cajun cooking relies heavily on seafood.*
Below: *Seafood Jambalaya (page 54).*

CONTENTS

INTRODUCTION

From Cajun Country, along the swamps and bayous of Southwest Louisiana, has come a style of cooking that is hearty, spicy and vibrant. It blends ancient French country cooking with influences as diverse as American Indian, African slave and Spanish Don.

The native Cajun is descended from early French colonists in Nova Scotia (which they called *L'Acadie* – 'an ideal rustic paradise'), who were driven out by the British in the mid-1700s. Those early Catholic refugees were offered a haven in Louisiana, then under Spanish rule. The Acadians – or Cajuns as they came to be called – developed a culture with its own customs, language (a French closer to Quebec than Paris), music and cooking, and this has remained intact for over 200 years.

The first Cajun settlers were wetlands farmers, trappers and fishermen. In the subtropical climate of Louisiana they found abundant seafood from the saltwater Gulf of Mexico and freshwater lakes and streams: crayfish (always called crawfish locally), shrimp, crab, oysters, frogs, eels, squid and many varieties of fish. They were also able to raise pigs and chickens, and grow succulent fruits and vegetables. Local crops such as rice – the staple starch – and corn, and plentiful game (duck, quail, partridge, pheasant, rabbit, armadillo, turtle, possum and muskrat) added to the culinary riches.

The local Indians taught the Cajuns many cooking secrets, such as using *filé* to flavor and thicken the now universally popular soup/stew Gumbo. The alternative thickener, okra, was brought by the slaves from Africa, and the African word for okra, *gombo*, gave the dish its name. The Spanish dish *paella* inspired a Cajun adaptation called Jambalaya. The Spanish may also have introduced the use of peppers, both sweet and hot.

At the same time, in New Orleans, the elegant Creoles (descendants of early French settlers, mostly colored) were enjoying their 'town' or 'city' style of cooking, with its rich sauces, fine pastries and sophisticated seasonings.

The blending of all these elements produced a native American cuisine that is unusual and soul-satisfying. The recipes in this book are mostly Cajun, with some popular Creole and other Southern specialties thrown into the pot. There are also some new dishes inspired by traditional cocktails and cuisine from New Orleans.

Making a roux

Many Cajun dishes are based on a roux, a mixture of oil or butter and flour cooked for 20-30 minutes till a rich brown color. The roux gives a full body and a rich flavor to the dish. These tips will help in making a roux:

● A heavy pot, traditionally cast iron, is the best to use as it will conduct the heat gently and evenly.
● The oil should be hot before the flour is added, gradually.
● The roux must be stirred constantly (with a long-handled spoon) to prevent burning or separating.
● When the desired color is reached, the vegetables (traditionally onions, garlic, celery and green pepper) are added to stop the roux browning further. These vegetables are best prepared ahead of time so you can give your undivided attention to the roux.

A note about ingredients

Crawfish are very cheap in Louisiana and are used extensively – and in great quantity – in Cajun cooking. Ideally they should be fresh – raw or just blanched (briefly cooked) – but elsewhere, only frozen crawfish may be available, and these are an acceptable substitute. *Crawfish 'fat'*, the orange substance in the heads, is picked out and sold separately from the tail meat. This fat adds richness to a crawfish dish, but it is not an essential ingredient. Cleaned crawfish shells for stuffing and heads stuffed with chopped crawfish meat, vegetables and bread crumbs are also sold.

Andouille sausage is a locally-made pork sausage with a strong smoky, garlicky taste. A recipe for homemade andouille is included in the book.

A *cushaw* is a squash that looks like a giant zucchini.

A *mirliton* is a pale green vegetable of the cucumber family that resembles a large pear. It is also called chayote or vegetable pear.

Filé is powdered dried wild sassafras leaves.

Pickapeppa sauce is a sweet spicy sauce from Jamaica.

Typically three kinds of *pepper* – black, white and red (cayenne) – are used to achieve the right balance of peppery flavor in a dish. These should, of course, be as freshly ground as possible. In addition, Tabasco sauce (from Avery Island, Louisiana), crushed dried red pepper flakes and chili powder add their own special warmth. Seasonings in the recipes can be adjusted according to personal taste.

Using this book

All recipes serve four unless otherwise stated.
All spoons are level spoons.

Chicken Maque Choux (page 34).

SOUPS

SEAFOOD FILÉ GUMBO

½ cup corn oil or lard
⅓ cup all-purpose flour
1 large onion, peeled and chopped
¼ cup chopped scallions
1-2 garlic cloves, peeled and minced
1 celery stalk, chopped
16-oz can whole peeled tomatoes in tomato juice
1 tablespoon tomato paste
2 tablespoons chopped parsley
1 teaspoon dried thyme
1 bay leaf
8 allspice berries
4 cloves
1 teaspoon salt
¼ teaspoon black pepper
¼ teaspoon white pepper
¼-½ teaspoon cayenne
2 tablespoons lemon juice
2 quarts cold water
2 cups white lump crabmeat
several small whole crabs, cleaned, or cracked crab claws
1 lb uncooked medium shrimp, peeled and deveined
1½-2 tablespoons filé powder

Heat the oil in a large, heavy pan and add the flour. Cook, stirring, to make a medium-brown roux (the color of peanut butter). Add the onion, scallions, garlic and celery and cook until softened. Add the tomatoes with their juice, breaking them down with the side of a spoon, then add the tomato paste, parsley, thyme, bay leaf, allspice, cloves, salt, peppers, cayenne to taste, lemon juice and water. Bring to a boil, stirring well. Add half the crabmeat and the whole crabs or claws.

Simmer for 1½-2 hours, stirring occasionally.

If liked, scoop out the allspice, cloves and bay leaf. Add the shrimp and the remaining crab and simmer for a further 15 minutes.

Remove the pan from the heat and stir in enough filé powder to thicken. Do not boil the gumbo after adding the filé powder. Serve hot.

NOTE: Other seafood, such as purged crawfish, lobster and well-scrubbed clams may be added to the gumbo, as available. Cooked seafood may be used, too. The finished gumbo will not have the richness of flavor given by the crab cooked in it, but will still be delicious. Just heat cooked seafood through in the finished sauce.

SERVES 4-6

GUMBO Z'HERBES

2 lb mixed green leaves, such as collard greens, mustard greens, turnip greens, beet, carrot or radish tops, spinach, green cabbage, chicory, lettuce, watercress, parsley, scallion tops
¼ cup bacon fat or corn oil
⅓ cup all-purpose flour
1 large onion, peeled and chopped
1 garlic clove, peeled and minced
1 green pepper, cored, seeded and diced
1 bay leaf
½ teaspoon dried thyme
1-1½ teaspoons salt
¼ teaspoon black pepper
¼ teaspoon white pepper
¼-½ teaspoon cayenne
½ lb smoked ham, cut into chunks
½ lb garlic sausage, cut into chunks

Wash the greens thoroughly and drain. Chop them coarsely, discarding any tough center stems. Put the greens in a large kettle with 1 cup cold water (do this in batches if necessary). Cover, bring to a boil and cook until the greens are wilted – 5-15 minutes depending on type. Drain, reserving the liquid. Add enough water to the liquid to yield 1½ quarts.

Heat the fat or oil in a heavy pot, add the flour and cook, stirring, about 15-20 minutes or until the roux is medium brown (the color of peanut butter). Add the onion, garlic and green pepper and cook 5-10 minutes or until softened, stirring occasionally.

Stir in the measured liquid with the bay leaf, thyme, salt, peppers and cayenne to taste. Add the greens, ham and sausage and mix well. Bring to a boil, then simmer for 1½-2 hours, stirring occasionally.

Discard the bay leaf, and taste and adjust the seasoning before serving, over rice.

NOTE: Homemade andouille sausage may be used instead of the garlic sausage called for here. Cook it before adding to the gumbo.

Seafood Filé Gumbo.

SERVES 4-6

CHICKEN AND OKRA GUMBO

⅓ cup corn oil
¼ cup all-purpose flour
1 large onion, peeled and chopped
1-2 garlic cloves, peeled and minced
1 small green pepper, cored, seeded and
　diced
1 celery stalk, diced
1 lb fresh okra, trimmed and very finely
　sliced
1½ tablespoons chopped fresh parsley
1 bay leaf
½ teaspoon dried thyme
1 teaspoon salt
¼ teaspoon black pepper
¼ teaspoon white pepper
¼ teaspoon cayenne
Tabasco or other hot pepper sauce
½ lb ripe, flavorsome tomatoes, coarsely
　chopped (peeled if necessary)
½ cup tomato purée
6 cups chicken stock or water
3-lb chicken, cooked
1½ cups fresh corn kernels

Heat the oil in a large heavy pan and add the flour. Cook over a low heat, stirring, to make a dark-brown roux (the color of hazelnut shells). Add the onion, garlic, green pepper and celery and cook until lightly browned, stirring occasionally. Add the okra, parsley, bay leaf, thyme, salt, peppers, and cayenne and Tabasco to taste, then stir in the tomatoes, tomato purée and half the stock or water. Bring to a boil, stirring well. Simmer for 1½ hours, stirring occasionally. During this time, the okra, which is initially slimy, will turn the mixture very dark and glutinous.

Meanwhile, remove the chicken meat from the carcass. Discard all skin and cut the meat into bite-sized pieces.

Add the chicken meat and corn to the gumbo with the remaining stock or water and simmer for 30 minutes longer, stirring from time to time.

SERVES 4-6

FISH COUBOUILLON

½ cup corn oil or bacon fat
½ cup all-purpose flour
2 large onions, peeled and chopped
2 garlic cloves, peeled and finely chopped
1 celery stalk, chopped
½ green pepper, cored, seeded and chopped
16-oz can chopped tomatoes in tomato juice
⅓ cup tomato paste
2½ cups fish stock or water
½ cup dry red wine
2 teaspoons salt
¼ teaspoon black pepper
¼ teaspoon white pepper
¼-½ teaspoon cayenne
2 tablespoons lemon juice
2 bay leaves
½ teaspoon dried thyme
2 lb skinless, firm fish fillets (catfish, redfish,
　monkfish, turbot, halibut or haddock), cut
　into large chunks
3 tablespoons chopped fresh chives or green
　scallion tops
2 tablespoons chopped fresh parsley

Heat the oil in a large heavy pan, add the flour and cook, stirring, to make a medium-brown roux (the color of peanut butter). Add the onions, garlic, celery and green pepper and cook until softened, stirring occasionally.

Stir in the tomatoes with their juice, the tomato paste, stock or water, wine, salt, peppers, cayenne to taste, lemon juice, bay leaves and thyme. Bring to a boil, then simmer for 30 minutes, stirring frequently.

Add the fish chunks and simmer 10 minutes longer.

Sprinkle over the chives and parsley and serve hot.

SERVES 6-8

CRAWFISH BISQUE

½ cup corn oil or bacon fat
⅓ cup all-purpose flour
1 large onion, peeled and chopped
1-2 garlic cloves, peeled and finely chopped
1 celery stalk with leaves, chopped
4 large scallions, white and green parts
    chopped separately
1 quart water
¼ cup tomato paste
1 teaspoon dried thyme
1 bay leaf
6 tablespoons chopped fresh parsley
8 allspice berries
3 cloves
1 teaspoon salt
¼ teaspoon black pepper
¼ teaspoon white pepper
¼-½ teaspoon cayenne
2 tablespoons lemon juice
3 lb uncooked crawfish tails, with fat if
    available
hot freshly cooked rice

Heat the oil in a large, heavy pan. Add the flour and cook, stirring, to make a medium-brown roux (the color of peanut butter). Add the onion, garlic, celery and white parts of the scallions and cook until softened, stirring occasionally.

Gradually stir in the water, then add the tomato paste, thyme, bay leaf, 4 tablespoons of the parsley, the allspice, cloves, salt, peppers, cayenne to taste and the lemon juice. Bring to a boil, stirring well.

Chop about one-quarter of the crawfish tails and add with the fat, if available. Cover and simmer for 1 hour, stirring occasionally.

Add the remaining whole crawfish tails and simmer, covered, for 15 minutes longer.

Stir in the green parts of the scallions and the remaining parsley. Serve hot over rice in soup plates.

NOTE: If available, add 12 or more stuffed crawfish heads (thawed if frozen) 5 minutes before serving.

SERVES 6-8

Crawfish Bisque.

SCALLION VICHYSOISSE

2 tablespoons butter
1 small onion, peeled and chopped
1½ cups chopped scallions
2 medium potatoes (about ½ lb), peeled and
    chopped
2 cups hot water
1 cup milk
1 cup heavy cream or sour cream
2 tablespoons lemon juice
salt and white pepper
Tabasco or other hot-pepper sauce
chopped fresh chives for garnish

Melt the butter in a saucepan and add the onion and scallions. Cover and sweat gently for about 10 minutes or until very soft but not colored. Add the potatoes and water and bring to a boil. Cover again and simmer for 30 minutes. Let cool.

Purée the soup in a blender or food processor and pour into a large mixing bowl. Add the milk, cream, lemon juice, and salt, pepper and Tabasco to taste. Cover closely and chill well.

Serve garnished with chives or scallion tops.

SERVES 4-6

OYSTER STEW

6 tablespoons butter
6 scallions, white and green parts finely
    chopped separately
¼ cup finely chopped celery
1 small garlic clove, peeled and minced
3 tablespoons all-purpose flour
2 cups milk
1 cup heavy cream
⅛-¼ teaspoon cayenne
salt and white pepper
3 dozen oysters (1-1¼ lb), shucked and
    liquor reserved
2 tablespoons dry sherry wine

Melt the butter in a heavy saucepan and cook the white part of the scallions, the celery and garlic until softened. Stir in the flour and cook for 2 minutes, then gradually stir in the milk and cream. Bring to a boil, stirring. Add the cayenne and salt and pepper to taste. Simmer 10 minutes, stirring frequently.

Meanwhile, in another saucepan cook the oysters in their liquor until just firm – 2-3 minutes

Strain the oyster liquor into the 'stew' and stir in well. Stir in the sherry, and taste and adjust the seasoning. Fold in the oysters, and serve hot, sprinkled with the green scallion tops.

NOTE: Be sparing with the salt as the oyster liquor may be salty.

SERVES 4-6

FRENCH ONION SOUP

4 tablespoons butter
1 lb large white onions, peeled and thinly
    sliced
1½ tablespoons all-purpose flour
3½ cups beef stock, preferably homemade
½ cup dry red wine
1 tablespoon Worcestershire sauce
salt and black pepper
8 slices of French bread, each ½-inch thick
2-3 tablespoons olive oil or melted butter
2 garlic cloves, halved
¼ cup freshly grated Parmesan cheese

Preheat the oven to 350°.

Melt the butter in a large, heavy saucepan, add the onions and cook gently, covered, for about 20-25 minutes or until soft and golden, stirring occasionally. Sprinkle over the flour and stir in well. Cook 2-3 minutes. Stir in the stock, wine, Worcestershire sauce, and salt and pepper to taste. Bring to a boil, stirring, then simmer 20-30 minutes.

Meanwhile, brush the bread slices on both sides with oil or melted butter and arrange on a baking sheet. Toast in the oven for 10-15 minutes or until golden and crisp. Rub with the cut sides of the garlic while the bread is still warm; discard the garlic. Set the bread aside.

Put two slices of bread in each bowl and ladle over the soup. Sprinkle with the cheese and serve.

Oyster Stew.

RED BEAN SOUP

2 cups dried red kidney beans, soaked
  overnight and drained
2 tablespoons butter
1 large onion, peeled and chopped
1 garlic clove, peeled and minced
1 large celery stalk with leaves, chopped
1 carrot, peeled and chopped
½ lb smoked ham, cut into large chunks
1 large ham bone (if available)
2 quarts water
1 tablespoon Worcestershire sauce
2 tablespoons chopped fresh parsley
½ teaspoon dried thyme
2 bay leaves
2 tablespoons lemon juice
⅛ teaspoon dried hot red pepper flakes
salt and black pepper
chopped fresh parsley for garnish

Put the beans in a saucepan, cover with fresh water and bring to a boil. Boil for 10 minutes and drain. Set aside.

Melt the butter in a Dutch oven or very large saucepan and cook the onion, garlic, celery and carrot, covered, until softened. Add the beans, ham, ham bone, water, Worcestershire sauce, parsley, thyme, bay leaves, lemon juice, pepper flakes, and salt and pepper to taste. Bring to a boil and simmer 2 hours or until the beans are very soft.

Discard the ham bone. Scoop out the chunks of ham and reserve.

Press the soup through a fine sieve and return it to the saucepan. Discard the solids in the sieve. Cut the chunks of ham into small dice and add to the soup. Reheat, and taste and adjust the seasoning. Serve hot, sprinkled with a little parsley.

SERVES 4-6

APPETIZERS

HOT PEANUTS

3 tablespoons corn oil
2 garlic cloves, peeled and minced
1-3 teaspoons dried hot red pepper flakes
¼-½ teaspoon cayenne
salt
1 lb shelled peanuts, skinned

Preheat the oven to 300°.

Heat the oil in a saucepan and add the garlic, pepper flakes, and cayenne and salt to taste. Stir for 1 minute, then stir in the peanuts.

Pour the peanut mixture onto a baking sheet and toast in the oven for 20-25 minutes, stirring occasionally, until lightly golden.

Drain well and leave to cool on paper towels.

MARINATED SHRIMP

½ cup olive or salad oil
2 tablespoons red wine vinegar
2 tablespoons lemon juice
1 teaspoon Worcestershire sauce
½ teaspoon salt
⅛ teaspoon black pepper
⅛ teaspoon white pepper
¼ teaspoon cayenne
¼ cup chopped scallions
1-2 garlic cloves, peeled and halved
½ sweet red pepper, cored, seeded and cut
    into short fine strips
1 teaspoon drained capers, chopped
1 celery stalk, thinly sliced crosswise
2 lb large cooked shrimp, peeled and
    deveined
4 lettuce leaves (optional)

Combine the oil, vinegar, lemon juice, Worcestershire sauce, salt, peppers and cayenne in a mixing bowl. Lightly beat together with a wire whisk.

Add the scallions, garlic, sweet pepper, capers and celery and stir to mix. Fold in the shrimp.

Cover closely and marinate in the refrigerator for at least 3 hours.

Discard the garlic before serving. If desired, serve in lettuce-leaf cups.

DEEP-FRIED OYSTERS WITH HOT SAUCE

¾ cup yellow cornmeal
⅛-¼ teaspoon cayenne
salt and black pepper
2 dozen oysters, shucked and drained
oil for deep frying
Hot Sauce:
½ cup mayonnaise, preferably homemade,
    or half mayonnaise and half sour cream
3 tablespoons prepared horseradish,
    preferably freshly grated
2 teaspoons Dijon mustard
⅛ teaspoon mustard powder
¼ teaspoon sugar
salt and white pepper
1-2 tablespoons lemon juice

Mix together the ingredients for the sauce. Cover closely and refrigerate for several hours to allow the flavors to blend.

Mix the cornmeal with cayenne, salt and pepper to taste. Dredge the oysters in the cornmeal. Deep fry in batches in oil heated to 375° for about 2 minutes or until golden brown. Drain on paper towels and serve immediately, with the Hot Sauce.

SERVES 4-6

Left: Marinated Shrimp.

HOT CRABMEAT DIP

8 oz cream cheese
2 tablespoons butter
⅔ cup light beer
½ lb white crabmeat, flaked
½ cup chopped scallions
⅛-¼ teaspoon cayenne
Tabasco or other hot pepper sauce
salt and white pepper

Shrimp and Mirliton Rémoulade.

Combine the cream cheese, butter and beer in a heavy saucepan or the top of a double boiler and melt over a gentle heat. When smooth, add the crabmeat, scallions and seasonings to taste. Heat through.

Serve in a cheese fondue pot or chafing dish, with an assortment of crackers for dipping.

NOTE: As the dip is being kept hot while eaten, it may be necessary to stir in another tablespoon or so of beer to keep the consistency dippable.

SERVES 4-6

CRÊPES AUX FRUITS DE LA BAYOU

1 cup all-purpose flour
½ teaspoon salt
1 large egg, beaten
1¼ cups milk
oil for frying
Filling:
4 tablespoons butter
6 tablespoons all-purpose flour
1 garlic clove, peeled and minced
½ cup chopped scallions
⅓ cup diced celery
1 cup fish stock, preferably homemade, or bottled clam juice
1 cup milk
½ cup dry vermouth or white wine
4 freshly shucked oysters, chopped and liquor reserved
2 tablespoons chopped fresh parsley
½ teaspoon dried thyme
½ teaspoon mustard powder
⅛-¼ teaspoon Tabasco or other hot pepper sauce
salt and white pepper
½ lb peeled cooked ocean or bay shrimp
½ lb white lump crabmeat
½ cup heavy cream

Sift the flour and salt into a mixing bowl. Add the egg and half the milk and beat until smooth. Gradually beat in the remaining milk.

Lightly oil and heat an 8-inch crêpe pan or skillet. Pour a small ladleful (about one-eighth) of the batter into the pan and tilt the pan so the batter covers the bottom evenly. Cook for about 1 minute or until the underside is lightly browned. Turn the crêpe and cook the second side for about 30 seconds to brown it lightly. Tip the crêpe out of the pan. Make seven more crêpes in the same way, adding more oil to the pan as necessary. Stack the crêpes with a piece of wax paper between each. Set aside.

To make the filling, melt the butter in a saucepan and stir in the flour. Cook for 2-3 minutes, stirring, then add the garlic, scallions and celery. Cook until softened, stirring occasionally. Add the stock, milk and vermouth or wine and bring to a boil, stirring well. Add any liquor from the oysters. Simmer until thickened.

Stir in the parsley, thyme, mustard powder, and Tabasco, salt and pepper to taste. Simmer gently for 15 minutes, stirring frequently.

Preheat the oven to 350°.

Add the shrimp, crabmeat and oysters to the filling and heat through. Stir in the cream.

Fill the crêpes generously with the filling and arrange them side by side in a buttered baking dish. Cover with foil and reheat in the oven for 20-30 minutes. Serve hot.

SERVES 4 or 8

SHRIMP AND MIRLITON RÉMOULADE

2 mirlitons (chayotes)
1½ lb cooked medium shrimp, peeled and deveined
cherry tomatoes
watercress
fresh tarragon or parsley sprigs for garnish
Sauce rémoulade:
1 cup mayonnaise, preferably homemade
2 teaspoons Dijon mustard
¼-½ teaspoon Worcestershire sauce
1½-2 tablespoons lemon juice or white wine vinegar
1 tablespoon drained capers, finely chopped
3 tablespoons finely chopped gherkin or dill pickle
2 tablespoons chopped mixed fresh parsley, chives and tarragon
2 teaspoons anchovy paste
salt and white pepper

First make the sauce. Mix together all the ingredients, adding Worcestershire sauce, lemon juice or vinegar, salt and pepper to taste. Cover and chill for at least 2 hours to allow the flavors to blend.

Cook the mirlitons in boiling water for 45 minutes to 1 hour or until tender. Drain and cool. Peel the mirlitons if necessary, cut them in half lengthwise and remove the seed, if any. Slice thinly lengthwise.

Arrange the shrimp and mirliton slices on individual serving plates with cherry tomatoes and watercress sprigs. Spoon over the sauce, and garnish with tarragon or parsley sprigs.

SERVES 6

OEUFS EN COCOTTE DIABLÉ

1 teaspoon mustard powder
6 tablespoons heavy cream
½ cup ground cooked ham
¼ teaspoon cayenne
salt and white pepper
4 large eggs

Preheat the oven to 350°.

Mix the mustard with 2 tablespoons of the cream. Add the ham, cayenne, and salt and pepper to taste and mix well.

Divide the ham mixture between four buttered ramekins or other small heatproof dishes such as custard cups, pressing the ham in an even layer over the bottom. Break an egg into each ramekin and top each with a spoonful of cream.

Place the ramekins on a baking sheet and bake for 10-15 minutes or until the whites of the eggs are set but the yolks are still runny.

Serve hot.

PETITES QUICHES LORRAINE

1 cup all-purpose flour
¼ teaspoon mustard powder
pinch of salt
6 tablespoons butter or margarine
3-4 tablespoons ice water
Filling:
¼ lb sliced bacon
1 cup grated Swiss or Gruyère cheese
3 large eggs
1-1¼ cups light cream or milk
Tabasco or other hot pepper sauce
⅛-¼ teaspoon cayenne
salt and white pepper

Sift the flour, mustard and salt into a bowl. Cut in the butter, then rub in until the mixture resembles fine crumbs. Bind to a dough with the water. Wrap and chill for 20 minutes.

Preheat the oven to 375°.

Roll out the dough and use to line 6 fluted tartlet tins, each measuring 3 inches across the base.

Fry the bacon in a skillet until crisp and rendered of fat. Drain on paper towels and crumble.

Divide the bacon and cheese between the pastry cases. Lightly beat together the eggs, cream or milk and Tabasco, cayenne, salt and pepper to taste. Pour into the pastry cases. Arrange on a baking sheet.

Bake about 20-25 minutes or until puffed and golden brown. Serve warm or cold.

MAKES 6

CHEESE PUFFS

1 cup water
4 tablespoons butter
½ cup all-purpose flour
½ cup grated sharp cheese
pinch of mustard powder
pinch of hot paprika
pinch of cayenne
pinch of salt
2 large eggs, beaten
Filling:
8 oz cream cheese, at room temperature
2 tablespoons Pickapeppa sauce
¼ cup diced pimiento
1 tablespoon capers, finely chopped

Preheat the oven to 375°.

Put the water and butter in a heavy saucepan and heat to melt the butter. Bring to a boil, then remove from the heat and beat in the flour all at once. Beat in the cheese and seasonings until smooth and the mixture forms a ball. Gradually beat in the eggs to make a smooth, glossy dough.

Drop the dough in blobs from a heaped teaspoon onto a buttered baking sheet. Bake for 20-25 minutes or until risen, golden brown and crisp. Make a slit in the side of each puff to allow the steam to escape, then return to the turned-off oven to keep hot.

To make the filling, beat the cream cheese with the Pickapeppa sauce, then mix in the pimiento and capers.

Pipe or spoon the filling into the cheese puffs and serve hot.

MAKES 20-24

VARIATION: For an alternative filling, combine 6 oz cream cheese with Tabasco or other hot pepper sauce to taste and mix in ½ cup finely chopped cooked shrimp and ¼ cup chopped scallions.

Petites Quiches Lorraine (left); Cheese Puffs (right).

PORK PÂTÉ WITH CREOLE SAUCE

1 lb lean ground pork
1 lb pork liver, ground
½ lb pork fat, ground
2 garlic cloves, peeled and minced
½ cup dry red wine
2 teaspoons salt
½ teaspoon black pepper
½ teaspoon white pepper
½ teaspoon cayenne
2 teaspoons dried thyme
Sauce:
1 large ripe, flavorsome tomato, seeded and
    diced
2-3 scallions, finely chopped
1 celery stalk, diced
½ sweet red pepper, cored, seeded and diced
3 tablespoons tomato purée
1 tablespoon lemon juice
Tabasco or other hot pepper sauce
salt and white pepper

Preheat the oven to 300°.

Combine the pork, liver, pork fat, garlic, wine, salt, peppers, cayenne and thyme in a mixing bowl and mix together thoroughly with the hands. Pack into a 5-cup capacity loaf pan.

Place the loaf pan in a roasting pan and pour boiling water into the roasting pan to come about 1 inch up the sides of the loaf pan. Bake in this water bath in the oven for 1½-2 hours or until the pâté has shrunk from the sides of the pan and is well browned.

Remove from the water bath, pour off excess fat from the pan and cool. Cover the pâté with foil and weight it down with heavy cans of food or similar weights. Refrigerate overnight.

Mix together the sauce ingredients with Tabasco, salt and pepper to taste. Serve the pâté sliced, with the sauce.

SERVES 6-8

Andouille Sausage Salad (left); Pork Pâté with Creole Sauce (right).

ANDOUILLE SAUSAGE SALAD

½ lb homemade andouille sausage (see page
    42), cut into 8 slices
assorted salad greens, such as arugula,
    radicchio, Belgian endive, chicory, field
    lettuce, red leaf lettuce, etc.
5 tablespoons olive oil
4 scallions, chopped
3 tablespoons red wine vinegar
¼ - ½ teaspoon sugar
½ teaspoon mustard powder
salt and black pepper

Fry the slices of sausage in a hot skillet for about 10 minutes on each side or until browned and cooked through.

Meanwhile, wash and dry the salad greens and divide them between four individual serving plates.

Place the sausage on top of the greens and set aside. Add the oil to the sausage fat in the skillet and heat. Add the scallions and fry for 1-2 minutes or until softened. Stir in the vinegar, sugar, mustard, and salt and pepper to taste and heat for 30 seconds, stirring with a wire whisk.

Pour the hot dressing over the sausage and greens and serve immediately.

ACADIAN STUFFED MUSHROOMS

8-12 large open mushrooms (total weight
    about 1¼-1½ lb)
2 tablespoons butter
¼ cup finely chopped onion
1 garlic clove, peeled and minced
¼ lb bulk pork sausage
⅛ teaspoon dried thyme
1 tablespoon chopped fresh parsley
pinch of ground allspice
pinch of cayenne
pinch of dried hot red pepper flakes
salt and black pepper
dash of Liquid Smoke
2 tablespoons fine fresh bread crumbs,
    preferably from French bread
2 tablespoons grated Parmesan cheese
½ teaspoon hot paprika

Preheat the oven to 400°.

Remove the mushroom stems and chop them finely. Set the caps aside.

Melt half the butter in a small skillet and cook the chopped mushroom stems, onion and garlic until softened and excess liquid has evaporated. Remove from the heat and add the sausage, thyme, parsley, allspice, cayenne, pepper flakes, salt and pepper to taste and Liquid Smoke. Mix well.

Stuff the mushroom caps with the pork mixture and arrange them side by side in an oiled baking dish. Mix together the bread crumbs, cheese and paprika and sprinkle over the stuffing. Dot with the remaining butter.

Bake about 20 minutes, basting once or twice with the juices in the dish. Serve hot.

MAIN DISHES

FILETS DE POISSON PLAQUEMINE

1 tablespoon olive oil
1 small onion, peeled and chopped
1 garlic clove, peeled and minced
1 celery stalk, chopped
½ green pepper, cored, seeded and chopped
16-oz can chopped tomatoes in tomato juice
1 teaspoon sugar
½ teaspoon dried hot red pepper flakes
1 teaspoon Worcestershire sauce
salt and black pepper
1 lb collard greens
2 tablespoons butter
1-2 teaspoons cornstarch
½ cup grated Swiss or Gruyère cheese
1½-2 lb skinless fish fillet, cut into 4 portions

Heat the oil in a saucepan and cook the onion, garlic, celery and green pepper until softened. Add the tomatoes with their juice, sugar, pepper flakes, Worcestershire sauce and salt and pepper to taste. Bring to a boil, then simmer gently for approximately 30 minutes, stirring occasionally.

Preheat the oven to 350°C.

While the sauce is simmering, prepare the greens. Cut out thick stems, then shred the greens into very fine strips. Cook in boiling water until tender. Drain well, pressing out all excess liquid. Add the butter and salt and pepper to taste and toss together. Spread the greens in an even layer over the bottom of a baking dish.

Strain the sauce in a sieve, pressing through as much of the vegetables as possible. Return the sauce to the pan and thicken with the cornstarch mixed to a paste in a little cold water. Remove from the heat and cool slightly, then stir in the cheese.

Arrange the pieces of fish on top of the greens and cover with the sauce. Bake for about 20 minutes or until the fish flakes easily when tested with a fork. Serve hot.

CRAWFISH PIE

2 cups all-purpose flour
½ teaspoon salt
10 tablespoons (1¼ sticks) butter or margarine
6-8 tablespoons ice water
Filling:
6 tablespoons butter
¼ cup all-purpose flour
½ cup finely chopped onion
1 garlic clove, peeled and minced
⅓ cup finely chopped green pepper
¼ cup finely chopped celery
¼ cup chopped white scallion bulbs
½ tablespoon tomato paste
½ cup heavy cream
2 tablespoons dry vermouth or sherry wine
½ teaspoon salt
¼ teaspoon white pepper
⅛-¼ teaspoon cayenne
Tabasco or other hot pepper sauce
1½ lb peeled uncooked crawfish tails, halved if large
2 tablespoons chopped fresh parsley
¼ cup chopped green scallion tops

Preheat the oven to 350°.

Sift the flour and salt into a bowl. Cut and rub in the butter until the mixture resembles fine crumbs, then bind to a dough with the ice water. Wrap and chill while making the filling.

Melt the butter in a heavy saucepan and stir in the flour. Cook, stirring constantly, until a light-golden roux is formed. Add the onion, garlic, green pepper, celery and scallion bulbs and cook, stirring frequently, until softened. Stir in the tomato paste, cream, vermouth or sherry, salt, pepper, and cayenne and Tabasco to taste. Add the crawfish and stir to mix. Cover and cook gently for 5 minutes.

Meanwhile, divide the dough into two portions, one slightly larger than the other. Roll out the larger portion on a lightly floured surface and use to line an 8 or 9 inch pie pan. Dampen the pastry rim with a little cold water.

Mix the parsley and scallion tops into the crawfish filling, then spoon into the piecrust. Spread out evenly. Roll out the remaining dough and lay over the filling. Press the edges together and seal by fluting or pressing with the tines of a fork. Make several slits in the top crust.

Bake for 40-45 minutes or until the pastry is crisp and golden brown. Serve hot.

NOTE: If using frozen crawfish, be sure they are thawed and well drained before adding to the filling.

SERVES 4-6

Crawfish Pie.

PAN-FRIED CATFISH

1 cup fine yellow cornmeal
1 teaspoon salt
½ teaspoon black pepper
⅛-¼ teaspoon cayenne
4-8 catfish fillets (depending on size)
milk or buttermilk
1 cup corn oil

Mix the cornmeal with the salt, pepper and cayenne on a sheet of wax paper. Dip the fish fillets in milk or buttermilk to coat, then dredge in the cornmeal mixture.

Heat about half the oil in a heavy skillet until very hot. Add some of the fish and fry for 3-5 minutes on each side or until golden brown. Drain on paper towels and keep hot. Heat the remaining oil and fry the rest of the fish. Serve hot.

VARIATIONS: Other fish fillets, particularly trout, may be cooked in the same way.

ROULADES AUX PALOURDES

4 bacon slices
¼ cup finely chopped onion
2 tablespoons finely chopped green pepper
2 tablespoons finely chopped celery
1 cup minced clams
1 cup dry white wine
½ teaspoon salt
¼ teaspoon white pepper
⅛-¼ teaspoon cayenne
8 or 16 Boston lettuce leaves, depending on size
8 skinless sole fillets (1¼-1½ lb total weight)
Tabasco or other hot pepper sauce

Preheat the oven to 350°.

Fry the bacon in a skillet until browned and rendered of fat. Remove and drain on paper towels, then crumble. Set aside.

Pour off all but 1 tablespoon of bacon fat from the skillet. Add the onion, green pepper and celery and cook until softened. Remove from the heat and add the clams, 1-2 tablespoons of the wine, the salt, pepper and cayenne to taste. Mix well together. Let cool briefly.

Put the lettuce leaves in a mixing bowl and pour over boiling water to cover. Leave to blanch for 1 minute, then drain and rinse in cold water. Drain again and spread out on a dish towel to dry.

Lay the sole fillets out on a flat surface and divide the clam stuffing between them. Spread it over evenly, then roll up the fillets. Wrap each roll in one or two lettuce leaves. Pack the rolls into a buttered baking dish and pour over the remaining wine. Bake for 20 minutes.

Using a slotted spoon, remove the rolls from the baking dish and drain on paper towels. Arrange on a serving platter and keep hot.

Pour the cooking liquid into a saucepan and boil until reduced to about ½ cup. Add Tabasco to taste and strain over the rolls. Serve hot.

BROILED SPICED SALMON FILLETS

8 salmon fillets (about 1½-2 lb total weight)
6 tablespoons butter, melted
1 tablespoon lemon juice
¾ teaspoon salt
⅛ teaspoon black pepper
⅛ teaspoon white pepper
⅛-¼ teaspoon cayenne

Preheat the broiler.

Arrange the fish fillets, skin side down, in a shallow buttered pan, in one layer if possible.

Mix the butter with the lemon juice and drizzle over the fish. Combine the salt, peppers and cayenne to taste and sprinkle over the fish.

Broil about 4-5 inches from the source of heat for 10-12 minutes without turning. Baste once with the spicy butter in the pan. Serve hot, with lemon wedges.

STUFFED FISH IN RICH RED SAUCE

3-5 lb whole fish such as redfish, red snapper or black bass, boned and head removed if desired
Sauce:
¼ cup corn oil
3 tablespoons all-purpose flour
1 onion, peeled and finely chopped
1 garlic clove, peeled and minced
16-oz can chopped tomatoes in tomato juice
2 tablespoons tomato paste
1 cup water
salt and black pepper
Tabasco or other hot pepper sauce
dried hot red pepper flakes
Stuffing:
1 cup white crabmeat
½ cup fresh bread crumbs, preferably from French bread
¼ cup chopped fresh parsley
½ cup chopped scallions
1 large egg, beaten
salt and white pepper

Heat the oil in a heavy saucepan and add the flour. Cook, stirring, to make a medium-brown roux (the color of peanut butter). Add the onion and garlic and cook until softened. Stir in the tomatoes with their juice, tomato paste, water, and salt, pepper, Tabasco and pepper flakes to taste. Bring to a boil and simmer for 30 minutes, stirring occasionally.

Meanwhile, make the stuffing. Combine the crabmeat, crumbs, parsley, scallion, egg, and salt and pepper to taste.

Preheat the oven to 350°.

Stuff the fish with the crabmeat mixture. If desired, close the opening with two or three wooden toothpicks. Place the fish in a long, buttered pan and pour over the tomato sauce. Bake for 30-35 minutes or until the fish will flake easily when tested with a fork.

SERVES 6-8

Broiled Spiced Salmon Fillets.

CAJUN POPCORN

1 large egg
5 tablespoons milk
1 cup all-purpose flour or fine yellow
    cornmeal
1 teaspoon salt
¼ teaspoon black pepper
¼ teaspoon cayenne
1 lb peeled uncooked crawfish tails
oil for deep frying

Lightly beat the egg with the milk in a shallow dish. Mix the flour or cornmeal with the salt, pepper and cayenne on a sheet of wax paper or in a plastic bag. Dip the crawfish in the egg mixture, then coat with the seasoned flour or cornmeal.

Deep fry in oil heated to 375° until golden brown. Drain on paper towels and serve hot.

CRAWFISH ETOUFFÉE

6 tablespoons butter
1 onion, peeled and finely chopped
1 large garlic clove, peeled and minced
2 celery stalks, finely chopped
¼ cup finely chopped green scallion tops
¼ cup all-purpose flour
2 lb peeled uncooked crawfish tails, with fat
    if available
1 teaspoon salt
¼ teaspoon black pepper
⅛-¼ teaspoon cayenne
2 tablespoons chopped fresh parsley
1 tablespoon lemon juice
1½ cups water
1 lb potatoes, peeled and cut into 1 inch
    pieces

Melt the butter in a heavy saucepan and add the onion, garlic, celery and scallion tops. Cover and sweat over a low heat for 15-20 minutes, stirring occasionally.

Stir in the flour and cook, uncovered, for 2 minutes, stirring well.

Add the crawfish fat, if available, and cook 5 minutes longer, stirring constantly.

Add the remaining ingredients, with the crawfish, and stir to mix. Bring to a boil, then cover and simmer gently for 20-25 minutes or until the potatoes are tender and the crawfish are cooked. Serve hot.

VARIATION: Use 2 lb peeled and deveined uncooked large or jumbo shrimp instead of crawfish.

CRAWFISH BOIL

3-5 lb live crawfish
4 quarts water
¾ cup salt
1 teaspoon cayenne
1 teaspoon allspice berries
1 teaspoon cloves
1 teaspoon dried thyme
1 teaspoon black peppercorns
4 bay leaves
6 lemons, halved
2 large onions, peeled and quartered
1 head garlic, separated into cloves, unpeeled
2 celery stalks, chopped with leaves
1½ lb small red potatoes, scrubbed.

If necessary, purge the crawfish by soaking them in cold salted water for 15-20 minutes. Drain and repeat the soaking until the water is completely clear and no longer muddy.

Combine the water, salt, cayenne, allspice, cloves, thyme, peppercorns, bay leaves, squeezed lemon halves and the juice, onions, garlic and celery in a large kettle. Bring to a boil and simmer 20 minutes.

Add the potatoes and simmer 10 minutes longer.

Add the live crawfish, with more boiling water if necessary so they are just covered. Bring back to a boil and simmer for 7-15 minutes, depending on size, until cooked.

Allow to cool for 20 minutes, then serve warm, with the vegetables. Alternatively, cool completely and serve chilled.

VARIATION: Cook live crabs, lobster or shrimp in the same way.

Stuffed Butterflied Shrimp.

STUFFED BUTTERFLIED SHRIMP

24 uncooked large or jumbo shrimp (about
   2 lb in shell), peeled and deveined
4 tablespoons olive oil
½ cup finely chopped onion
⅓ cup chopped scallions
1 garlic clove, peeled and minced
⅓ cup finely chopped green pepper
¼ cup finely chopped celery
1 cup fresh bread crumbs, preferably from
   day-old French bread
¼ cup dry vermouth
½ cup diced tomato
1 teaspoon tomato paste
salt and white pepper
Tabasco or other hot pepper sauce
hot paprika

Preheat the oven to 400°.

Cut down the back or upper curved edge of a shrimp, not cutting all the way through, then open up like a book to make a butterfly shape. Butterfly the remaining shrimp.

Heat half the oil in a small skillet and cook the onion, scallions, garlic, green pepper and celery until softened but not browned. Remove from the heat.

Moisten the crumbs with the vermouth, squeezing them so they absorb the liquid. Add to the vegetables with the tomato, tomato paste, and salt, pepper and Tabasco to taste. Mix well.

Divide the stuffing between the shrimp, heaping it on top and pressing to firm. Arrange the shrimp, in one layer, in an oiled baking dish and drizzle over the remaining oil. Sprinkle with a little paprika.

Bake for 15 minutes or until golden brown and the shrimp are cooked. Serve hot.

GOUJONETTES

all-purpose flour
salt and black pepper
cayenne
2 large eggs
2 tablespoons water
about 1½ cups fine dry bread crumbs
1½ lb skinless sole or flounder fillets, cut
   into ½ inch wide fingers
oil for deep frying

Season the flour with salt, pepper and cayenne to taste. Spread out on a sheet of wax paper or put into a plastic bag. Lightly beat the eggs with the water in a shallow dish. Spread out the crumbs on a sheet of wax paper.

Lightly dredge the strips of fish in seasoned flour, then dip into the egg mixture and finally coat with crumbs. Deep fry in batches in oil heated to 375° until golden brown. Drain on paper towels and serve hot.

SHRIMP AND CRAB WITH SAUCE PIQUANT

⅓ cup corn oil
¼ cup all-purpose flour
1 large onion, peeled and chopped
1-2 garlic cloves, peeled and minced
1 celery stalk, chopped
½ green pepper, cored, seeded and chopped
½ sweet red pepper, cored, seeded and
    chopped
1 cup chopped ripe, flavorsome tomatoes
    (peeled if necessary)
1 cup tomato purée
1 cup dry white wine
1 cup fish stock or water
2 tablespoons chopped fresh parsley
2 bay leaves
½ teaspoon dried thyme
½ teaspoon dried basil
¼ teaspoon grated nutmeg
½ teaspoon ground allspice
2 teaspoons dark brown sugar
strip of finely peeled lemon rind
1 teaspoon salt
¼ teaspoon black pepper
¼ teaspoon white pepper
¼-½ teaspoon cayenne
1 lb uncooked medium shrimp, peeled and
    deveined
1 lb white lump crabmeat

Heat the oil in a large, heavy pan and add the flour. Cook, stirring, to make a medium-brown roux (the color of peanut butter). Add the onion, garlic, celery and peppers and cook until golden brown, stirring occasionally. Add the tomatoes, tomato purée, wine, stock or water, parsley, bay leaves, thyme, basil, nutmeg, allspice, sugar, lemon rind, salt, peppers and cayenne to taste. Bring to a boil, stirring well, then simmer for 45 minutes to 1 hour or until the sauce is rich and thick.

Add the shrimp and crab. Cover and simmer for 10 minutes longer or until the shrimp are cooked and the crab is hot. Do not stir too much or the crabmeat will separate into flakes.

BLACKENED REDFISH

1 teaspoon salt
½ teaspoon black pepper
½ teaspoon white pepper
½-¾ teaspoon cayenne
½ teaspoon dried thyme
½ teaspoon dried oregano
1½-2 teaspoons hot paprika
½ teaspoon hot chili powder
4 skinless redfish fillets, about ½ lb each,
    ½-¾ inch thick
1½ sticks butter, melted

Mix together the salt, peppers, cayenne to taste, thyme, oregano, paprika to taste and chili powder in a small bowl.

Heat a heavy black cast-iron skillet over high heat until it is extremely hot. This will take about 5 minutes.

Dip the fish fillets in the melted butter, then sprinkle both sides evenly with the seasoning mix and pat it on. Put two fillets in the hot skillet and pour 1 teaspoon butter over each (the butter may flame up, so stand well back). Cook about 1½-2 minutes or until charred, then turn the fillets over, pour another 1 teaspoon butter over each and cook for a further 1½-2 minutes or until the second side is charred and the fish is cooked through.

Remove the fish from the skillet and keep hot. Cook the remaining fillets in the same way. Pour any remaining melted butter over the fish and serve immediately.

NOTE: It is essential to have good ventilation in the kitchen when cooking this dish as the burning spices will emit strong fumes.
VARIATIONS: Other fish fillets such as pompano, red snapper and tilefish can be prepared in the same way.

OLD-FASHIONED ACADIAN CLAM AND POTATO PIE

1-1½ dozen softshell clams, scrubbed
2 lb potatoes, peeled and grated
¼ lb bacon, chopped
salt and black pepper
cayenne

Shrimp and Crab with Sauce Piquant.

Steam the clams until they open. Remove them from their shells, reserving the liquor, and chop finely. Set aside.

Preheat the oven to 375°.

Wring out the potatoes, a handful at a time, in cheesecloth or doubled all-purpose kitchen cloth. Do this over a bowl to catch the liquid. Put the wrung-out potatoes in another bowl.

Measure the potato liquid and discard it. Measure the clam liquor and add enough dry white wine or water to it to make it the same quantity as the discarded potato water. Bring this liquid to a boil and gradually stir in the potatoes. They will absorb the liquid. Remove from the heat.

Fry the bacon in a skillet until crisp and golden (do not overbrown). Remove with a slotted spoon and set aside. Pour the bacon fat into a baking dish measuring about 8 inches square. Make a layer of half the potatoes on the bottom, season well with salt, pepper and cayenne, and cover with the clams. Spread over the rest of the potatoes and season as before. Sprinkle the bacon on top.

Bake for 1¼-1½ hours or until the top is brown and crisp. Serve hot or warm.

VARIATIONS: Canned minced clams may be used instead of fresh clams, and bottled clam juice or fish stock instead of fresh clam liquor.

OYSTER PIE

1½ cups milk
¼ cup finely chopped celery
1 bay leaf
strip of thinly peeled lemon rind
6 tablespoons butter
1 cup sliced mushrooms
¼ cup all-purpose flour
½ cup oyster liquor or dry white wine
½ teaspoon salt
¼ teaspoon white pepper
⅛ teaspoon cayenne
1 pint freshly shucked oysters
2 cups hot mashed potatoes
3 tablespoons finely chopped green scallion
    tops

Preheat the oven to 400°.

Combine the milk, celery, bay leaf and lemon rind in a saucepan and scald the milk. Remove from the heat, cover and leave to infuse for 20 minutes.

Meanwhile, melt 2 tablespoons of the butter in another saucepan and cook the mushrooms until they are wilted. Remove the mushrooms with a slotted spoon and set aside.

Add the remaining butter to the pan and melt it, then stir in the flour and cook, stirring, for 2 minutes. Strain the milk and add to the pan with the oyster liquor or wine. Bring to a boil, stirring, and simmer until thickened. Add the salt, pepper and cayenne, then stir in the oysters and mushrooms.

Pour the oyster mixture into an oval baking dish that measures about 12×8 inches. Pipe or spread the mashed potatoes over the top, sealing in the oyster filling. Sprinkle over the scallion tops and press them gently into the potato. Dot with the remaining butter.

Bake for 20-30 minutes or until the top is golden brown and the filling is bubbling. Serve hot.

VARIATIONS: Scallops or chunks of a firm-fleshed fish such as monkfish can be used instead of oysters, or a combination of seafood can be used.

Barbecued Shrimp.

BARBECUED SHRIMP

½ cup dry white wine
2 sticks butter
1 tablespoon lemon juice
1 teaspoon finely grated lemon rind
8 allspice berries
6 cloves
1-2 garlic cloves, peeled and minced
2 bay leaves
1 tablespoon fresh thyme leaves, or
   1 teaspoon dried thyme
2 teaspoons chopped fresh rosemary leaves,
   or ½ teaspoon dried rosemary
½ teaspoon dried hot red pepper flakes
salt and black pepper
2 lb uncooked medium or large shrimp in
   shell, deveined if preferred

Put all the ingredients except the shrimp in a saucepan and bring to a boil. Remove from the heat, cover and leave to infuse for 20 minutes.

Preheat the oven to 400°.

Mix the shrimp with the sauce and pour into a baking pan. Bake for 15 minutes or until the shells turn pink, stirring occasionally. Serve hot.

CHICKEN WITH OYSTER AND ARTICHOKE STUFFING

4-lb chicken with giblets
1 carrot, peeled and chopped
1 celery stalk with leaves, chopped
1 small onion, peeled and quartered
few black peppercorns
4 tablespoons butter
1 tablespoon Pickapeppa sauce
1 tablespoon all-purpose flour
Stuffing:
1 cup long-grain rice
1 cup dry white wine
3 tablespoons butter
8- to 9-oz package frozen artichoke hearts,
   thawed, or 14-oz can artichoke hearts,
   drained
½ cup chopped scallions
½ cup chopped canned smoked oysters
Tabasco or other hot pepper sauce
salt and black pepper
1 large egg, beaten

Put the chicken giblets in a saucepan and add the carrot, celery, onion, peppercorns and 3 cups of water. Bring to a boil, then half cover and simmer for 1 hour. Strain the stock, and discard the vegetables. Reserve 2 cups of stock.

Cook the rice in 1 cup of the giblet stock and the wine, covered, for 15-20 minutes or until the rice is tender and all liquid has been absorbed. Add the butter and toss to coat the rice. Cool.

Preheat the oven to 350°.

Chop the artichoke hearts and add to the rice with the scallions, oysters, and Tabasco and salt and pepper to taste. Bind with the egg.

Use about two-thirds of the stuffing to stuff the vent end of the chicken. Close the opening with a skewer or sew with a trussing needle and thread. Cream the butter and Pickapeppa sauce together, using a fork. Loosen the skin over the breast of the chicken by wriggling your fingers up between the skin and flesh. Spread half the spiced butter over the breast meat under the skin, then pack in the remaining stuffing. Close the neck opening with a skewer or trussing needle and thread.

Place the chicken in a roasting pan and spread the remaining spiced butter all over it. Roast for 1½-2 hours or until the bird is cooked.

Transfer the chicken to a warmed serving platter and keep hot. Pour off all but 1 tablespoon of the fat from the pan. Add the flour to the pan and stir well to mix with the fat and sediments. Stir in the remaining 1 cup giblet stock and bring to a boil on top of the stove, stirring constantly. Simmer for 2-3 minutes. Taste and adjust the seasoning. Serve this gravy with the chicken.

CHICKEN ROLLS WITH CRAWFISH STUFFING

3 tablespoons butter
1 onion, peeled and finely chopped
1 garlic clove, peeled and minced
¼ green pepper, cored, seeded and diced
¼ sweet red pepper, cored, seeded and diced
2 tablespoons chopped fresh parsley
¼ teaspoon dried thyme
1 teaspoon salt
¼ teaspoon black pepper
¼ teaspoon white pepper
¼ teaspoon cayenne
pinch of ground allspice
1 cup fine fresh bread crumbs, preferably
    from day-old French bread
1 cup dry white vermouth
1 cup chopped cooked crawfish meat
1 large egg, beaten
8 skinless, boneless chicken breast halves
1 tablespoon olive oil
½ cup heavy cream

Melt 2 tablespoons of the butter in a small skillet and cook the onion, garlic and peppers until softened. Remove from the heat and stir in the parsley, thyme, salt, peppers, cayenne and allspice. Moisten the bread crumbs with ¼ cup of the vermouth and add to the mixture with the crawfish meat and egg. Mix well together.

Place a chicken breast between two sheets of wax paper and pound with a heavy skillet or meat mallet until thin. Pound the remaining breasts in the same way.

Divide the stuffing between the breasts, spreading it out evenly and leaving a border clear all around. Roll up the breasts from a short end, tucking in the sides, and tie into shape with string or secure with wooden toothpicks.

Heat the remaining butter and the oil in a heavy skillet in which all the rolls will fit comfortably. Add the rolls and brown on all sides. Add ½ cup of the remaining vermouth, cover and cook for 15-20 minutes longer, turning the rolls once or twice.

Remove the rolls and keep hot. Add the remaining ¼ cup vermouth to the skillet and stir to mix with the juices and sediment. Strain the liquid into a small saucepan. Stir in the cream and boil until the liquid has reduced to a sauce-like consistency, about 3-4 minutes. Taste and adjust the seasoning.

Serve the sauce with the chicken rolls (string or wooden picks removed).

FROGS' LEGS WITH FRENCH QUARTER SAUCE

12 large pairs frogs' legs
milk
¼-½ teaspoon Tabasco or other hot pepper
    sauce
all-purpose flour
salt and black pepper
1 cup corn oil
Sauce
6 canned anchovy fillets, well drained
milk
1 tablespoon butter
1 tablespoon olive oil
1-2 garlic cloves, peeled and minced
16-oz can chopped tomatoes in tomato juice
⅓ cup chopped scallions
black pepper
Tabasco or other hot pepper sauce

First make the sauce. Soak the anchovy fillets in milk to cover for 5-10 minutes (to remove excess saltiness). Drain and pat dry with paper towels, then chop finely.

Heat the butter and oil in a small saucepan and cook the garlic and anchovies gently, mashing until well broken down. Add the tomatoes with their juice and simmer 15 minutes, stirring occasionally.

Stir in the scallions, and pepper and Tabasco to taste. Simmer 5 minutes longer or until thick. Keep hot.

Dip the frogs' legs in milk spiced with Tabasco, then coat with flour seasoned with salt and pepper. Heat the corn oil in a wide, heavy skillet and fry the frogs' legs for 3-5 minutes on each side or until golden brown and tender. Drain on paper towels and serve hot, with the sauce.

SHRIMP-STUFFED CORNISH GAME HENS

4 Rock Cornish game hens
2 tablespoons butter, melted
¼ teaspoon black pepper
¼ teaspoon white pepper
Stuffing:
2 tablespoons butter
1 small onion, peeled and finely chopped
1 small garlic clove, peeled and minced
1 celery stalk, diced
1 cup crumbled cornbread
1 cup cooked peeled ocean or bay shrimp
1 tablespoon chopped fresh parsley
¼ teaspoon dried thyme
¼ teaspoon dried hot red pepper flakes
½ teaspoon salt
2 tablespoons lemon juice
½ large egg, beaten

To make the stuffing, melt the butter in a small skillet and cook the onion, garlic and celery until softened. Remove from the heat and add the remaining stuffing ingredients. Mix well and cool.

Preheat the oven to 350°.

Stuff the hens and truss them. Arrange in a roasting pan. Mix the melted butter with the peppers and brush over the hens. Roast for 1¼-1½ hours, basting occasionally with the juices in the pan.

Shrimp-stuffed Cornish Game Hens.

CHICKEN MAQUE CHOUX

8 ears fresh corn, shucked
3 tablespoons corn oil
4-lb chicken, cut up
2 onions, peeled and finely chopped
1 small green pepper, cored, seeded and
    diced
1 lb ripe, flavorsome tomatoes, chopped
    (peeled if necessary)
1 teaspoon sugar
½ teaspoon dried basil
salt and black pepper
¼-⅓ cup milk

Cut the kernels from the ears of corn; there should be about 3 cups. Scrape the ears with the back of a knife to obtain the milky liquid. Set the kernels and liquid aside.

Heat the oil in a wide shallow pan and brown the chicken pieces on all sides. Remove them. Add the onions and cook until softened. Return the chicken, and add the corn and liquid, green pepper, tomatoes, sugar, basil, and salt and pepper to taste. Cook for 30 minutes, stirring occasionally, until the chicken is tender. Add a little of the milk from time to time if the mixture seems too dry.

NOTE: If fresh corn is not available, frozen corn may be used instead, with 2 tablespoons milk or heavy cream in place of the corn liquid.

CANARD POIVRÉ

5-lb duck
2 teaspoons salt
1 teaspoon black pepper
1 teaspoon white pepper
¾ teaspoon cayenne
½ teaspoon hot paprika

Preheat the oven to 400°. Prick the duck skin all over so the fat will be released during cooking. Try not to pierce the meat.

Mix together the seasonings and rub all over the duck, inside and out. Reserve the remaining seasoning mixture. Truss the duck and place it on a rack in a roasting pan. Roast for 1 hour.

Pour off all the fat from the pan. Replace the duck in the pan, without the rack. Sprinkle over the remaining seasoning mixture. Roast for 30-45 minutes longer. To test if the duck is done, pierce a meaty part with a skewer; the juices should be only faintly pink.

Let the duck rest for 10-15 minutes before carving. The juices in the roasting pan, skimmed of excess fat, can be served with the duck.

SMOTHERED CHICKEN BREASTS

½ teaspoon salt
¼ teaspoon white pepper
¼ teaspoon cayenne
6-8 chicken breast halves
¼ lb sliced bacon
1 onion, peeled and sliced
2 carrots, peeled and cut into short sticks
¼ lb button mushrooms, sliced
1 tablespoon all-purpose flour
1 cup chicken stock
½ cup milk
1 tablespoon lemon juice
1 tablespoon Worcestershire sauce
½ teaspoon dried thyme
1 bay leaf
¼ teaspoon ground allspice
⅛ teaspoon grated nutmeg

Preheat the oven to 350°.

Mix together the salt, pepper and cayenne and rub all over the chicken breasts. Set aside.

Cook the bacon in a flameproof casserole until browned and rendered of fat. Remove the bacon using tongs and set aside. Add the chicken to the casserole and brown in the bacon fat. Remove the chicken and set aside.

Add the onion, carrots and mushrooms to the casserole and cook until the onion is softened. Sprinkle over the flour and stir in well, then add the stock and milk. Add the lemon juice, Worcestershire sauce, thyme, bay leaf, allspice and nutmeg. Bring to a boil, stirring.

Return the chicken to the casserole and turn to coat with the liquid. Crumble the bacon and sprinkle over the top. Cover and transfer to the oven. Bake about 1 hour.

Transfer the chicken breasts and vegetables to a serving plate and keep hot. Skim the fat from the surface of the cooking liquid and boil to reduce it if necessary. Spoon the liquid over the chicken and serve.

Canard Poivré.

SOUTHERN FRIED CHICKEN WITH CREAM GRAVY

2 eggs
3 tablespoons milk
few drops of Tabasco or other hot pepper
    sauce
2 2-lb chickens, cut up
all-purpose flour
corn oil or bacon fat for frying
Gravy:
2 tablespoons all-purpose flour
1½ cups milk
½ cup heavy cream
salt and black pepper
hot paprika

Lightly beat the eggs with the milk and Tabasco. Coat the chicken pieces with this mixture, then dredge in flour.

Heat oil or fat about 1 inch deep in a large skillet until it is very hot (about 350°). Add the chicken pieces, in batches if necessary, and brown well on all sides, turning them with tongs. Pack all the browned chicken pieces in the skillet, cover and reduce the heat to moderate. Cook for about 30 minutes longer, turning the pieces once or twice, until the chicken is tender.

Remove the chicken pieces, drain well on paper towels and keep hot.

Pour off all but 2 tablespoons oil or fat from the skillet, retaining the sediment and browned bits of coating. Add the flour and cook, stirring, about 3 minutes or until browned. Stir in the milk and cream and bring to a boil, stirring well. Add salt, pepper and paprika to taste. Simmer about 5 minutes.

Serve the chicken with the gravy.

CHICKEN IN SAUCE PIQUANT

1 teaspoon salt
½ teaspoon black pepper
½ teaspoon cayenne
3- to 4-lb chicken, cut up
½ cup corn oil
⅓ cup all-purpose flour
1 large onion, peeled and chopped
1-2 garlic cloves, peeled and minced
1 green pepper, cored, seeded and chopped
1 large celery stalk, chopped
16-oz can chopped tomatoes in tomato juice
1 cup tomato purée
2 tablespoons chopped fresh parsley
½ teaspoon dried thyme
1 bay leaf
½ cup dry red wine

Mix together the salt, pepper and cayenne. Rub the spice mixture all over the chicken pieces; reserve the leftover spice mixture.

Heat the oil in a heavy skillet in which the chicken pieces will fit comfortably. Add the chicken and brown briskly on all sides. Remove the chicken and set aside.

Add the flour and the rest of the spice mixture to the oil in the skillet. Reduce the heat to low and cook, stirring constantly, for about 15 minutes or until the roux is medium-brown (the color of peanut butter). Add the onion, garlic, green pepper and celery and cook about 5 minutes or until softened, stirring occasionally.

Stir in the tomatoes with their juice, tomato purée, herbs, wine and 1 cup water. Bring to a boil. Return the chicken pieces to the skillet, cover and simmer gently for about 40 minutes, stirring from time to time.

Uncover the skillet and simmer for 15-20 minutes longer or until the sauce is rich and thick. Taste and adjust the seasoning, and discard the bay leaf before serving.

SQUAB EN CASSEROLE

2 tablespoons corn oil
4 squabs, cleaned
¼ lb Canadian bacon, cut into strips
1 onion, peeled and finely chopped
1 garlic clove, peeled and minced
1 celery stalk, diced
¼ cup bourbon
1 cup game or chicken stock
2 teaspoons tomato paste
2 tablespoons chopped fresh parsley
1 tablespoon chopped fresh marjoram, or
    1 teaspoon dried marjoram
1 bay leaf
salt and black pepper
½ lb mushrooms, sliced
1 cup seedless green grapes
1 tablespoon butter, at room temperature
2 tablespoons all-purpose flour

Preheat the oven to 350°

Heat the oil in a skillet and brown the squabs on all sides. Remove them to a flameproof casserole. Add the bacon, onion, garlic and celery to the skillet and cook until golden brown. Add to the casserole.

Pour the bourbon into the skillet and bring to a boil, stirring in the sediment and browned bits on the bottom of the pan. Add the stock, tomato paste, parsley, marjoram, bay leaf, and salt and pepper to taste. Bring to a boil, then pour into the casserole. Add the mushrooms. Shake the casserole to distribute the ingredients evenly around the squabs. Cover and cook in the oven for 30 minutes.

Add the grapes, cover again and cook 30 minutes longer.

Remove the squabs to a serving plate and keep hot. Place the casserole over heat on top of the stove and bring to a boil. Mash the butter with the flour to make a paste. Add in small pieces to the cooking liquid, stirring well until thickened. Taste and adjust the seasoning, and discard the bay leaf.

Spoon the sauce over the squabs and serve hot.

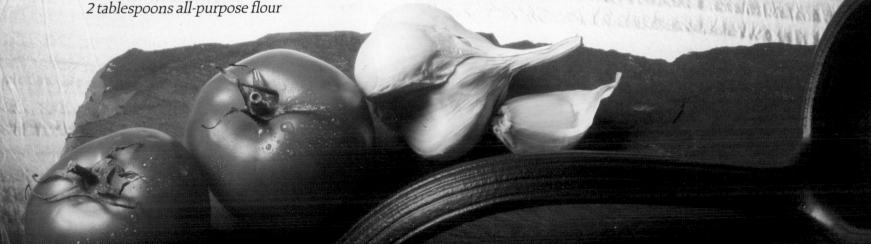

TURKEY, SAUSAGE AND PEPPER STEW

½ lb bulk pork sausage
1 large garlic clove, peeled and minced
3 tablespoons chopped fresh parsley
½ teaspoon dried hot red pepper flakes
½ cup fresh bread crumbs, preferably from
    day-old French bread
¼ teaspoon Liquid Smoke
salt and black pepper
about 4 tablespoons corn oil
all-purpose flour
cayenne
1½-2 lb skinless, boneless turkey breast, cut
    into 1-inch cubes
1 onion, peeled and sliced
1 green pepper, cored, seeded and sliced
1 sweet red pepper, cored, seeded and sliced
16-oz can whole peeled tomatoes in tomato
    juice
1 tablespoon red wine vinegar
½ cup turkey or chicken stock
1 teaspoon dried thyme
½ lb smoked pork sausage, thickly sliced

Preheat the oven to 350°.

Combine the pork sausage, garlic, parsley, pepper flakes, bread crumbs, Liquid Smoke, and salt and pepper to taste in a mixing bowl. Mix well together with the hands, then shape into eight balls.

Heat 2 tablespoons of the oil in a skillet and brown the sausage balls on all sides. Using a slotted spoon, transfer them to a casserole.

Season the flour with salt, pepper and cayenne to taste. Dredge the pieces of turkey in the seasoned flour. Add to the skillet, in batches, and brown on all sides. Add more oil as necessary. As the turkey pieces are browned, transfer them to the casserole.

Add the onion and peppers to the skillet and cook until the onion is softened. Add the tomatoes, breaking them down with the side of a spoon, then add the vinegar, stock and thyme. Bring to a boil.

Pour the vegetable mixture over the turkey and sausage balls in the casserole. Cover and cook in the oven for 30 minutes.

Add the smoked sausage and stir in. Cook for 30 minutes longer.

SERVES 4-6

Turkey, Sausage and Pepper Stew.

QUAILS IN WINE CREAM

8 quails
salt and black pepper
cayenne
2 tablespoons butter
2 tablespoons olive oil
1 small onion, peeled and finely chopped
1 small garlic clove, peeled and minced
1 small celery stalk, diced
8 juniper berries, lightly crushed
1 bay leaf, broken into pieces
1½ cups dry white wine
½ cup heavy cream

Rub the quails inside and out with salt, pepper and cayenne. Truss the birds.

Heat the butter and oil in a deep heavy skillet and brown the quails on all sides; remove and set aside. Add the onion, garlic and celery to the skillet and cook until softened, stirring occasionally.

Stir in the juniper berries, bay leaf and wine and bring to a boil. Return the quails to the skillet, cover tightly and simmer gently for 30 minutes or until the quails are cooked.

Remove the quails to a warmed serving platter and keep hot. Strain the cooking juices into a saucepan, pressing down on the vegetables and seasonings in the strainer to extract all the juice. Boil the liquid until reduced to 1 cup. Add the cream and boil until reduced to about 1 cup again. Taste and adjust the seasoning and spoon the sauce over the quails. Serve hot.

CHICKEN FRIED STEAK

1½-2 lb boneless beef top round steak, cut
  about ½ inch thick and trimmed of all fat
1 large egg
2 tablespoons milk
1 cup all-purpose flour or fine cracker or
  bread crumbs
salt and black pepper
6 tablespoons corn oil
1-2 tablespoons Worcestershire sauce

Pound the beef with a meat mallet or the side of a heavy plate to break down the fibers. Continue pounding with the mallet or the base of a heavy skillet until the meat is about ¼ inch thick.

Lightly beat the egg with the milk. Season the flour or crumbs with salt and pepper to taste.

If desired, cut the beef into four portions. Dip in the egg mixture to coat on all sides, then dredge lightly but evenly in the seasoned flour or crumbs.

Heat the oil in a large heavy skillet until very hot. Add the beef and brown well on both sides to make a good crust. Reduce the heat to low, add the Worcestershire sauce and cover the pan. Continue cooking 5-10 minutes or to the desired degree of doneness. Serve hot.

CAJUN MEATLOAF

1 lb lean ground round
½ lb lean ground pork
1 cup fine fresh bread crumbs, preferably
  from day-old French bread
1 large egg, beaten
1 small onion, peeled and finely chopped
3 tablespoons tomato purée
1 tablespoon Worcestershire sauce
½ teaspoon salt
¼ teaspoon black pepper
¼-½ teaspoon cayenne
1 teaspoon mustard powder
1 cup diced garlic sausage

Preheat the oven to 350°.

Combine the beef, pork, crumbs, egg and onion in a mixing bowl. In another bowl, mix together the tomato purée, Worcestershire sauce, salt, pepper, cayenne to taste and mustard. Add this seasoning mix to the meat and blend well together using the hands. Work in the garlic sausage.

Pack the mixture into a 5-cup capacity loaf pan. Bake for 1 hour or until well browned and shrunk slightly from the sides of the pan. Pour off excess fat before serving, hot or cold.

Chicken Fried Steak.

MARINATED RABBIT

½ cup cider vinegar
½ cup orange juice
1 cup water
1 small onion, peeled and sliced
1 garlic clove, peeled and minced
1 bay leaf
4 allspice berries, lightly crushed
4 cloves, lightly crushed
salt and black pepper
cayenne
3-lb rabbit, cut up
all-purpose flour
4-6 tablespoons corn oil
½ lb apples (2-3), peeled, quartered and cored
½ cup raisins
2 tablespoons redcurrant jelly

Combine the vinegar, orange juice, water, onion, garlic, bay leaf, allspice, cloves, and salt, pepper and cayenne to taste in a mixing bowl. Add the rabbit pieces and press down into the liquid. Cover and marinate overnight.

Preheat the oven to 350°.

Drain the rabbit, reserving the marinade, and pat dry. Dredge the pieces lightly in flour.

Heat 4 tablespoons oil in a heavy casserole and brown the rabbit pieces, in batches if necessary. Add more oil as required.

When all the rabbit pieces have been browned, return them to the casserole. Pour over the marinade and add the apple quarters and raisins. Bring to a boil.

Cover the casserole and cook in the oven for 1-1¼ hours or until the rabbit is tender. Stir from time to time, mashing the apple down into the cooking liquid.

Remove the rabbit pieces to a serving platter and keep hot. Place the casserole over heat on top of the stove and bring the cooking liquid to a boil. Add the redcurrant jelly and stir until it has melted. Taste and adjust the seasoning, then spoon over the rabbit and serve.

NOTE: Choose a tart yet sweet variety of apple that will break down in cooking.

BEEF-STUFFED EGGPLANT

4 eggplants, about ½-¾ lb each
1½ lb lean ground round
5 tablespoons butter
1 onion, peeled and finely chopped
1 garlic clove, peeled and minced
1 cup diced celery
1 cup diced green pepper ·
1 large ripe, flavorsome tomato, diced
2 tablespoons fresh thyme leaves, or
   1 teaspoon dried thyme
2 tablespoons Worcestershire sauce
salt and black pepper
1 large egg, beaten
2 tablespoons tomato paste
1 cup fine fresh bread crumbs, preferably
   from French bread

Preheat the oven to 375°.

Cook the eggplants in boiling water for 5-10 minutes or until they are just tender when tested with the point of a sharp knife. Drain. When cool enough to handle, cut the eggplants in half lengthwise and scoop out the flesh, leaving shells about ¼-inch thick. Set the shells aside. Chop the flesh.

Cook the beef in a skillet, without additional fat, until it is browned and crumbly. Pour it into a strainer to drain.

Melt 2 tablespoons of the butter in the skillet and cook the onion, garlic, celery and green pepper until softened. Add the eggplant flesh, beef, tomato, half the thyme, the Worcestershire sauce and salt and pepper to taste. Cook for a further 10 minutes, stirring occasionally.

Remove from the heat and mix in the egg and tomato paste.

Fill the eggplant shells with the beef mixture, mounding it up. Arrange in a greased baking dish. Mix the crumbs with the remaining thyme and sprinkle over the tops. Dot with the remaining butter. Bake for 15-20 minutes or until piping hot and browned and crisp on top. Serve hot.

DAUBE DE BOEUF LOUISIANE

¼ lb bacon, chopped
2 lb boneless beef chuck or round steak, cut
   into 1-inch cubes
1 large onion, peeled and chopped
1-2 garlic cloves, peeled and minced
1 celery stalk, chopped
½ green pepper, cored, seeded and cut into
   strips
½ sweet red pepper, cored, seeded and cut
   into strips
3 tablespoons all-purpose flour
16-oz can whole peeled tomatoes in tomato
   juice
½ cup red wine
½ cup beef stock or water
1 bouquet garni
1 teaspoon salt
½ teaspoon black pepper
⅛-¼ teaspoon cayenne
½ teaspoon mild chili powder
⅛ teaspoon dried hot red pepper flakes
1 teaspoon capers, coarsely chopped
¼ lb small button mushrooms
½ cup large white scallion bulbs

Preheat the oven to 325°.

Fry the bacon in a heavy skillet until crisp and rendered of fat. Using a slotted spoon, transfer the bacon to a casserole.

Pour off all but 2 tablespoons fat from the skillet, then add the beef cubes, in batches, and brown on all sides. As the beef is browned, transfer it to the casserole.

Add the onion, garlic, celery and peppers to the skillet and cook until softened, stirring occasionally. Sprinkle over the flour and stir in well. Cook until golden brown. Add the tomatoes with their liquid, breaking them up with the side of a spoon, the wine, stock or water, bouquet garni, salt, pepper, cayenne to taste, chili powder, pepper flakes and capers. Bring to a boil, stirring well, then pour into the casserole.

Cover and cook in the oven for 1 hour.

Add the mushrooms and scallions and stir well. Cook for 30 minutes longer or until the beef is tender. Serve hot.

SERVES 4-6

GRILLADES AND GRITS

1½-2 lb boneless veal round, cut into ¼-inch
    thick slices and trimmed of all fat
1½ teaspoons salt
½ teaspoon black pepper
¼ teaspoon white pepper
¼ teaspoon cayenne
½ teaspoon mustard powder
7 tablespoons corn oil
¼ cup all-purpose flour
1 large onion, peeled and chopped
1 garlic clove, peeled and minced
1 celery stalk, chopped
1 green pepper, cored, seeded and chopped
1 cup tomato purée
1 cup stock or water
1 bay leaf
2 tablespoons chopped fresh parsley
1 tablespoon Worcestershire sauce
2 cups hot freshly cooked grits

Cut the veal into pieces about 2-3 inches square. Mix together the salt, peppers, cayenne and mustard. Rub this seasoning mixture into the veal; reserve any leftover seasoning.

Heat 2 tablespoons oil in a deep skillet and brown the veal, in batches if necessary. As the veal is browned, remove it. Add the rest of the oil to the skillet with the flour and cook, stirring, to make a dark-brown roux (the color of hazelnut shells). Mix in all the sediment from the bottom of the pan as you stir. Add the onion, garlic, celery and green pepper and cook until golden brown, stirring occasionally.

Stir in the tomato purée, stock or water, bay leaf, parsley and Worcestershire sauce as well as any reserved seasoning mix. Bring to a boil.

Return the veal to the skillet and mix into the sauce. Cook gently for 1 hour, stirring occasionally.

Serve hot, with the grits.

Daube de Boeuf Louisiane.

BAYOU PORK PIE

1½ lb ground pork
1 small onion, peeled and chopped
1 garlic clove, peeled and minced
2 celery stalks, diced
3 tablespoons chopped fresh parsley
1½ teaspoons salt
¼ teaspoon black pepper
¼ teaspoon white pepper
½ teaspoon cayenne
⅛ teaspoon ground cloves or allspice
⅛ teaspoon grated nutmeg
2 tablespoons all-purpose flour
1 cup chicken stock or water
2 cups yellow cornmeal
5 cups water
3 tablespoons butter or bacon fat
1 tablespoon Worcestershire sauce

Cook the pork with the onion, garlic and celery in a heavy skillet until the pork is browned and crumbly and the vegetables are softened. Stir in the parsley, salt, peppers, cayenne, cloves or allspice and nutmeg. Cover and cook over a low heat for 20 minutes.

Preheat the oven to 400°.

Sprinkle the flour over the pork mixture and stir in well. Cook 1 minute, then stir in the stock or water. Remove from the heat and let cool briefly.

Combine the cornmeal, water, 2 tablespoons butter or bacon fat and the Worcestershire sauce in a saucepan and bring to a boil, stirring well. Cook until thickened, then reduce the heat to moderate and cook for a further 5 minutes, stirring occasionally. Remove from the heat and cool for 2 minutes.

Spread about two-thirds of the cornmeal mush over the bottom and up the sides of a buttered baking dish (about 12 × 8 inches). Spread the pork filling in the center and level the surface. Cover with the remaining mush and dot the top with the rest of the butter.

Bake for 45 minutes, and serve hot.

ANDOUILLE SAUSAGE

1½ lb lean boneless pork
½ lb pork fat
3 garlic cloves, peeled and minced
1 tablespoon salt
¼ teaspoon black pepper
¼ teaspoon cayenne
1 teaspoon dried hot red pepper flakes
1 teaspoon hot paprika
½ teaspoon dried thyme
pinch of ground allspice
pinch of grated nutmeg
2 teaspoons Liquid Smoke
2-2½ feet large pork sausage casings
   (optional)

Using the coarse blade of a meat grinder, grind the pork and fat. If preferred, the pork and fat may be ground in a food processor, in small batches and as briefly as possible.

Put the pork and fat in a mixing bowl and add the garlic, salt, pepper, cayenne, pepper flakes, paprika, thyme, allspice, nutmeg and Liquid Smoke. Mix together thoroughly using the hands. Cover very closely and refrigerate overnight to allow the flavors to blend.

If using sausage casings, rinse them well in cold water to remove any salt. Drain well and tie one end closed with string. Stuff the pork mixture into the casings using the attachment on an electric meat grinder.

Alternatively, shape the pork mixture into a sausage on a sheet of lightly oiled foil and wrap the foil around to keep the shape.

To cook, cut into ½-inch thick slices and dry-fry in a hot skillet for about 10 minutes on each side or until browned and crisp.

MAKES 2 lb

STUFFED PORK CHOPS

4 large pork chops, each about 1½-inches
  thick
1 teaspoon salt
¼ teaspoon black pepper
¼-½ teaspoon cayenne
¼ teaspoon mustard powder
½ teaspoon dried thyme
2 tablespoons butter
1 onion, peeled and finely chopped
1 garlic clove, peeled and minced
1 small green pepper, cored, seeded and
  finely chopped
1 cup ground smoked ham
½ cup crumbled cornbread
1 large egg, beaten

Preheat the oven to 375°.

Cut a pocket horizontally in each chop, almost to the bone. Mix together the salt, pepper, cayenne to taste, mustard and thyme. Rub this all over the chops and into the pockets. Reserve any leftover spice mixture.

Melt the butter in a skillet and cook the onion, garlic and green pepper until softened. Remove from the heat and mix in the ham, cornbread, egg and reserved spice mixture.

Using about half the ham mixture, stuff the pockets in the chops. Arrange the chops in an oiled baking dish and mound the remaining stuffing on top of them. Bake about 1 hour.

Serve hot, with a thin beef or pork gravy.

BLACKENED PEPPER STEAK

1 tablespoon black peppercorns
1 tablespoon dried green peppercorns
1 teaspoon dried hot red pepper flakes
½ teaspoon dried thyme
4 boneless sirloin or filet mignon steaks,
  6-8 oz each
2 tablespoons butter
2 tablespoons olive oil
1 cup sliced mushrooms
2 tablespoons bourbon
½ cup heavy cream
salt

Combine the black and green peppercorns, pepper flakes and thyme in a mortar and pound with a pestle until coarse-fine. Press this mixture on to both sides of the steaks.

Heat 1 tablespoon of butter with 1 tablespoon oil in a heavy skillet and cook the mushrooms until the liquid they have exuded has evaporated and the mushrooms are lightly browned. Remove and set aside.

Heat the remaining butter and oil in the skillet until hot. Add the steaks and cook briskly about 2 minutes on each side until well browned. Reduce the heat and continue cooking to the desired degree of doneness. Transfer the steaks to warmed plates and keep hot.

Pour off excess fat from the pan, retaining the sediment. Add the bourbon to the skillet and bring to a boil, stirring to mix in the sediment. Add the cream and bring back to a boil, stirring well. Stir in the mushrooms and reheat briefly. Add salt to taste, and spoon the sauce over the steaks. Serve hot.

SAUSAGES IN SAUCE PIQUANT

2 tablespoons corn oil
2 lb country sausage links
2 tablespoons all-purpose flour
1 onion, peeled and chopped
¼ cup chopped scallions
1 garlic clove, peeled and minced
1 small green pepper, cored, seeded and
    chopped
1 cup tomato purée
1 cup beer
½ cup chopped tomatoes
1-2 tablespoons Pickapeppa sauce
¼ teaspoon Tabasco or other hot pepper
    sauce
salt and black pepper
1½ cups chopped fresh pineapple

Heat the oil in a large heavy skillet and brown the sausages on all sides; remove them from the pan. Add the flour to the fat remaining in the skillet and cook, stirring, until a medium-brown roux is formed (the color of peanut butter). Add the onion, scallions, garlic and green pepper and cook, stirring, for about 5 minutes or until softened. Stir in the tomato purée, beer, tomatoes, Pickapeppa and Tabasco sauces, and salt and pepper to taste. Bring to a boil.

Return the sausages to the skillet. Cover and simmer for 15 minutes, stirring occasionally.

Stir in the pineapple and simmer 15 minutes longer. Serve hot.

OVEN-BARBECUED SPARERIBS

3½-4 lb meaty pork spareribs, cut into
    1-rib pieces
1 cup ketchup
½ cup water
1 tablespoon Worcestershire sauce
2 tablespoons light brown sugar
1 tablespoon Dijon Mustard
1 teaspoon salt
¼ teaspoon black pepper
¼ teaspoon white pepper
¼-½ teaspoon cayenne
⅛-¼ teaspoon dried hot red pepper flakes
few drops of Liquid Smoke

Preheat the oven to 450°.

Arrange the ribs in a lightly greased pan. Cover and bake for 45 minutes.

Meanwhile, combine the remaining ingredients in a saucepan and bring to a boil, stirring well.

Pour off the fat from the pan. Pour over the sauce. Reduce the oven temperature to 350° and bake for 40 minutes longer, turning the ribs from time to time. Spoon over any sauce in the pan when serving.

Creole Pork.

CREOLE PORK

⅓ cup all-purpose flour
½ teaspoon salt
¼ teaspoon black pepper
¼ teaspoon cayenne
pinch of hot paprika
pinch of mustard powder
8 pork cutlets
4 tablespoons corn oil
1 onion, peeled and chopped
1 garlic clove, peeled and minced
½ green pepper, cored, seeded and diced
½ sweet red pepper, cored, seeded and diced
1 celery stalk, diced
2 16-oz cans chopped tomatoes in tomato
   juice
1 tablespoon Worcestershire sauce
¾ cup water

Mix together the flour, salt, pepper, cayenne, paprika and mustard. Dredge the cutlets in the spiced flour, shaking off the excess. Reserve the leftover spiced flour.

Heat the oil in a shallow flameproof casserole wide enough to take the cutlets in one layer. Add the cutlets and brown them on both sides. Remove the pork and set aside.

Add the onion, garlic, peppers and celery to the casserole and cook, stirring occasionally, until golden. Stir in the reserved spiced flour, then add the tomatoes with their juice, Worcestershire sauce and water. Stir well and bring to a boil

Return the pork to the casserole. Cover and simmer gently for 1 hour, stirring occasionally.

PORK TENDERLOIN WITH SWEET POTATO AND APPLE

2 pork tenderloins, ¾-1 lb each
½ cup puréed orange-fleshed sweet potatoes
   (yams), preferably freshly cooked
1 teaspoon ground cinnamon
½ teaspoon grated orange rind
salt and black pepper
1 cup peeled and thinly sliced crisp apples
4-6 bacon slices
½ cup dry white wine or chicken stock
½ cup orange juice

Make a cut lengthwise down one of the pieces of pork, cutting about halfway into it. Open the pork like a book and place it, cut side down, between two sheets of plastic wrap. Pound with a flat meat mallet or the bottom of a heavy skillet until the pork has a rectangular shape and is about ¼-½ inch thick. Repeat with the second piece of pork.

Preheat the oven to 375°.

Mix together the sweet potato purée, cinnamon, orange rind, and salt and pepper to taste. Divide in half and spread one portion over each piece of pork, on the cut side. Top with the apple slices. Roll up each piece of pork, from a short end. Top the rolls with the bacon slices and tie into shape with string.

Put the two pork rolls in a small roasting pan and pour around the wine or stock and orange juice. Roast for about 45 minutes, basting occasionally with the juices in the pan.

To serve, discard the string and cut the pork into slices across the rolls. Serve with the pan juices.

SERVES 4-6

LOUISIANA-STYLE LAMB CHOPS

1 tablespoon butter
1 tablespoon oil
8 large lamb loin chops, trimmed of excess fat
1 onion, peeled and chopped
1 garlic clove, peeled and minced
1 green pepper, cored, seeded and chopped
16-oz can chopped tomatoes in tomato juice
½ cup red wine
2 tablespoons chopped fresh parsley
1 bay leaf
½ teaspoon dried thyme
½ teaspoon salt
¼ teaspoon black pepper
¼ teaspoon white pepper
⅛-¼ teaspoon cayenne
⅛ teaspoon dried hot red pepper flakes
8 black olives, pitted and sliced
1 tablespoon capers, chopped

Heat the butter and oil in a large skillet and brown the chops on both sides; remove. Add the onion, garlic and green pepper to the skillet and cook until softened. Stir in the tomatoes with their juice, the wine, parsley, bay leaf, thyme, salt, peppers, cayenne to taste, and pepper flakes. Bring to a boil, stirring well, then simmer for 10 minutes, stirring occasionally.

Stir in the olives and capers. Return the chops to the skillet and spoon the sauce over. Cover and simmer for 15-20 minutes or until the chops reach the desired degree of doneness.

VARIATION: This is also delicious made with veal chops – one per person.

SMOTHERED LAMB

1 cup red wine
¼ cup brandy
2 onions, peeled, halved and thinly sliced
2 carrots, peeled and thinly sliced
1 garlic clove, peeled and minced
1 large sprig of fresh rosemary
1 bay leaf
½ teaspoon dried thyme
strip of thinly peeled orange rind
1 teaspoon salt
½ teaspoon black pepper
2-2½ lb lean boneless lamb, cut into large chunks
2 tablespoons butter
2 tablespoons olive oil
¼ lb Canadian bacon, diced
¼ cup all-purpose flour
16-oz can chopped tomatoes in tomato juice
½ cup dried blackeye peas, soaked overnight and drained
¼ lb mushrooms, sliced
2 tablespoons tomato paste
1½ cups water

In a large bowl, combine the wine, brandy, onions, carrots, garlic, herbs, orange rind, salt and pepper. Add the lamb chunks and mix in well. Cover and marinate for at least 8 hours, turning the lamb occasionally.

Heat the butter and oil in a flameproof casserole or Dutch oven and cook the bacon until golden brown. Stir in the flour and cook for 3 minutes. Add the tomatoes with their juice and stir in well, then add the blackeye peas, mushrooms, tomato paste, water, and lamb with its marinade. Stir to mix.

Bring to a boil, then cover and simmer for 2 hours or until the lamb is tender. Stir from time to time during cooking.

Smothered Lamb (left), Nutty Orange Rice (page 49).

NEW ORLEANS ROAST LAMB

4- to 4½-lb leg of lamb
½ tablespoon salt
¼ teaspoon black pepper
¼ teaspoon white pepper
¼-½ teaspoon cayenne
1 teaspoon dried thyme
1-2 garlic cloves, peeled and cut into slivers
½ small onion, peeled and cut into small
   slivers
½ green pepper, cored, seeded and cut into
   small slivers
½ cup dry red wine

Preheat the oven to 450°.

Trim excess fat from the meat. Make small slits all over the meat using the point of a sharp knife. Mix together the salt, peppers, cayenne to taste and thyme and rub all over the meat, including into the slits. Insert the garlic, onion and pepper slivers into the slits.

Place the leg in a roasting pan and roast for 20 minutes, then reduce the oven temperature to 325° and continue roasting for 1¾-2 hours or until the lamb reaches the desired degree of doneness.

Remove the lamb to a carving board, cover and set aside to rest for about 15 minutes before carving.

Pour off the fat from the roasting pan. Add the wine and bring to a boil on top of the stove, stirring to mix in the sediments. Strain this gravy, if desired, and serve with the lamb.

SERVES 4-6

RICE AND BEANS

NUTTY ORANGE RICE

2 tablespoons butter
1 onion, peeled and finely chopped
1 cup long-grain rice
1 teaspoon grated orange rind
½ cup orange juice
1 cup chicken stock or water
salt and white pepper
⅓ cup coarsely chopped pecans or walnuts

Melt the butter in a saucepan and cook the onion until softened. Add the rice and stir well to coat each grain with the buttery mixture. Add the orange rind and juice, stock or water and salt and pepper to taste. Bring to a boil. Stir once, then cover and simmer over a very low heat for 15-20 minutes or until the rice is just tender and the liquid has been absorbed.

Meanwhile, toast the nuts under the broiler for 3-4 minutes, shaking the pan frequently to turn the nuts over and prevent burning.

Add the nuts to the rice and fold through. Serve hot.

CREOLE RICE

2 tablespoons corn oil
¼ cup finely chopped onion
1 small garlic clove, peeled and minced
¼ green pepper, cored, seeded and diced
¼ sweet red pepper, cored, seeded and diced
1 small celery stalk, diced
1 zucchini, diced
½ eggplant, diced
1½ cups long-grain rice
½ cup tomato purée
Tabasco or other hot pepper sauce
salt and white pepper
¼ cup chopped Hot Peanuts (see page 15), optional

Heat the oil in a saucepan and cook the onion, garlic, peppers and celery until softened. Add the zucchini and eggplant, then stir in the rice and cook, stirring, for 1 minute. Add 1 cup water, the tomato purée, and Tabasco, salt and pepper to taste. Bring to a boil, stir once, then cover and simmer gently for 15-20 minutes or until the rice is tender and all the liquid has been absorbed.

If using, stir in the hot peanuts just before serving.

SERVES 4-6

RICE AND OLIVE SALAD

1 cup long-grain rice
1¾ cups chicken stock
¼ cup salad oil
2 tablespoons lemon juice
1 teaspoon salt
¼ teaspoon black pepper
⅛-¼ teaspoon cayenne
½ teaspoon mustard powder
½ cup mayonnaise, preferably homemade
½ cup chopped scallions
¾ cup chopped celery
¼ cup chopped radishes
1 large dill pickle, diced
¾ cup quartered black olives
2 tablespoons chopped fresh parsley

Cook the rice in the chicken stock, covered, for 15-20 minutes or until the rice is tender and all liquid has been absorbed.

Meanwhile, mix together the oil, lemon juice, salt, pepper, cayenne to taste and mustard.

Add the hot rice to the dressing and toss to mix. Cool.

Add the remaining ingredients to the rice and mix well. Cover closely and chill well before serving.

Nutty Orange Rice (left),
Rice and Olive Salad (right),
Creole Rice (bottom).

Cassoulet.

DIRTY RICE

2 tablespoons bacon fat or corn oil
2 onions, peeled and finely chopped
1-2 garlic cloves, peeled and minced
1 green pepper, cored, seeded and finely
    chopped
1 celery stalk, finely chopped
1 cup finely chopped mushrooms
2 tablespoons chopped fresh parsley
½ lb chicken livers, diced
¼ lb ground or diced chicken giblets or
    ground lean pork
2 teaspoons Worcestershire sauce
½ teaspoon cayenne
salt and black pepper
4 tablespoons water
1½ cups long-grain rice

Heat the bacon fat or oil in a heavy pan and add the onions, garlic, green pepper, celery, mushrooms and parsley. Cook until lightly browned, stirring occasionally. Add the livers and giblets or pork and cook until they are browned, mashing and stirring frequently. Stir in the Worcestershire sauce, cayenne, and salt and pepper to taste. Cover and cook over a low heat for 20 minutes, stirring from time to time. If necessary, add a spoonful or two of water when needed.

Meanwhile, cook the rice in boiling salted water until tender. Drain. Add the rice to the 'dirty' mixture. Toss together and serve.

SERVES 4-6

RED BEANS AND RICE

*1 lb dried red kidney beans, soaked
    overnight and drained*
1 meaty ham bone
2½ quarts water
1 teaspoon black pepper
½-1 teaspoon cayenne
1 tablespoon Worcestershire sauce
2 onions, peeled and chopped
1-2 garlic cloves, peeled and minced
*1 large green pepper, cored, seeded and
    chopped*
2 celery stalks, chopped
½ cup chopped fresh parsley
2 bay leaves
½ teaspoon dried thyme
½ tablespoon salt
1 lb smoked or hot sausage, sliced or cubed
hot freshly cooked rice

Put the beans in a saucepan, cover with water and bring to a boil. Boil for 10 minutes, then drain.

Return the beans to the pan and add the ham bone, measured water, pepper, cayenne and Worcestershire sauce. Bring to a boil. Half cover and simmer for 30 minutes.

Add the onions, garlic, green pepper, celery, parsley, bay leaves, thyme and salt and stir to mix. Simmer gently, half covered, for 1 hour.

Stir in the sausage and simmer uncovered for 1-1½ hours longer or until the mixture is quite thick and the beans are tender.

Remove the ham bone. Cut the meat from the bone and cut it into chunks. Return the meat to the beans and stir well. Serve with hot rice.

NOTE: A mixture of sausages will make a more interesting dish.

SERVES 4-6

CASSOULET

1-2 tablespoons corn or olive oil
½ lb Canadian bacon, cut into chunks
2 onions, peeled and sliced
2-4 garlic cloves, peeled and finely chopped
1 lb boneless lean pork, cut into large chunks
1 lb boneless lean lamb, cut into large chunks
½ lb garlic sausage, sliced
1 cup dry white wine
1 cup tomato purée
2 bay leaves
1 teaspoon dried thyme
¼ cup chopped fresh parsley
1 tablespoon salt
1 teaspoon black pepper
½-1 teaspoon cayenne
*1 lb dried white navy beans, soaked
    overnight and drained*
1 quart water
*3 cups fresh bread crumbs, preferably from
    French bread*

Preheat the oven to 300°.

Heat the oil in a heavy skillet and fry the bacon chunks until browned on all sides. Using a slotted spoon, transfer the bacon to a large deep casserole.

Add the onions and garlic to the skillet, with more oil if necessary, and cook until softened. Add to the casserole.

Brown the pork, lamb and sausage, in batches, with more oil as necessary. As the meat is browned, transfer it to the casserole.

Pour the wine into the skillet and bring to a boil, stirring in the sediment and browned bits from the bottom of the pan. Add the tomato purée, bay leaves, thyme, parsley, salt, pepper and cayenne to taste. Pour into the casserole. Add the beans and water and mix the ingredients together.

Bring the contents of the casserole to a boil. Sprinkle over about 1 cup of the crumbs to make a layer on the surface, then place the casserole in the oven. Bake 45 minutes.

Press the crust that will have formed back into the bean mixture and stir well. Sprinkle over another 1 cup of the crumbs and bake 45 minutes longer.

Press the crust in again and sprinkle over the remaining crumbs. Bake for a further 1-1½ hours or until the beans and meat are very tender and a golden crust has formed on top. Serve hot.

SERVES 8

SPICY FRUIT PURLOO

2 tablespoons butter
½ cup finely chopped scallions
¼ cup finely chopped green pepper
1 cup long-grain rice
1 teaspoon salt
½ teaspoon white pepper
⅛ teaspoon cayenne
1½ cups water
1 cup diced country ham
1 cup diced fresh pineapple
¼ cup raisins

Melt the butter in a heavy saucepan and cook the scallions and green pepper until the scallions are softened. Add the rice, salt, pepper and cayenne and cook, stirring, for 1 minute. Stir in the water, ham, pineapple and raisins.

Bring to a boil, then cover and simmer for 15-20 minutes or until the rice is tender and all the liquid has been absorbed.

CHEESE AND GRITS SOUFFLÉ

2 cups milk
1 cup quick grits
2-4 tablespoons butter
1 cup grated sharp Cheddar cheese
¼ cup chopped fresh herbs (parsley, chives,
    marjoram or thyme)
½ cup chopped scallions
1 teaspoon salt
½ teaspoon white pepper
Tabasco or other hot pepper sauce
3 large eggs, separated

Preheat the oven to 375°.

Bring milk to a boil in a heavy saucepan with 2 cups water. Slowly stir in the grits. Reduce the heat, cover and cook for 4-5 minutes, stirring occasionally, until thick.

Remove from the heat. Add the butter, cheese, herbs, scallions, salt, pepper and Tabasco to taste. Stir until the butter and cheese have mixed smoothly into the grits. Stir in the egg yolks.

Beat the egg whites until stiff. Add 1-2 spoonfuls to the grits mixture and beat in, then fold in the remaining whites with a metal spoon. Spoon the mixture into a buttered 1½ quart casserole. Bake for 35-40 minutes or until risen and golden brown. Serve immediately.

SERVES 6

HOT BEAN SALAD WITH GARLIC SAUSAGE

2 16-oz cans cannellini, pinto or other white
    beans, drained and rinsed
½ cup chopped scallions
1-2 garlic cloves, peeled and minced
6 tablespoons olive oil
2-3 tablespoons red wine vinegar
2 tablespoons chopped fresh parsley
1 large ripe flavorsome tomato, chopped
½ sweet red pepper, cored, seeded and diced
salt and black pepper
Tabasco or other hot pepper sauce
dried hot red pepper flakes
½ lb garlic sausage, sliced or cut into chunks

Combine the beans, scallions, garlic, oil, vinegar, parsley, tomato, sweet pepper, and salt, pepper, Tabasco and pepper flakes to taste in a saucepan. Heat for 5-10 minutes, stirring occasionally.

Meanwhile, fry the sausage in a heavy skillet until golden brown. Drain the sausage on paper towels and mix into the hot bean salad. Serve hot.

Hot Bean Salad with Garlic Sausage (top); Spicy Fruit Purloo (bottom).

SEAFOOD JAMBALAYA

½ lb homemade andouille sausage (see page 42), cut into ½-inch thick slices, or use French garlic sausage, Polish kielbasa or similar
1 tablespoon butter
1 onion, peeled and chopped
4 large scallions, chopped
1 garlic clove, peeled and minced (optional)
½ green pepper, cored, seeded and chopped
½ sweet red pepper, cored, seeded and chopped
1 large celery stalk with leaves, chopped
1½ cups long-grain rice
2 tablespoons chopped fresh parsley
½ teaspoon dried thyme
1 bay leaf
1 teaspoon salt
⅛ teaspoon black pepper
⅛ teaspoon white pepper
¼-½ teaspoon cayenne
⅛ teaspoon ground allspice
pinch of grated nutmeg
½ teaspoon anchovy paste
16-oz can chopped tomatoes in tomato juice
2 cups fish stock or water
2 1-lb lobsters, cooked
¾-1 lb cooked medium shrimp, peeled and deveined
¾ cup canned smoked oysters

Fry the sausage slices in a large heavy pot about 5 minutes on each side. Remove and set aside.

Add the butter to the sausage fat and melt it, then cook the onion, scallions, garlic, peppers and celery until softened. Stir in the rice and cook for 1 minute, then add the parsley, thyme, bay leaf, salt, peppers, cayenne to taste, allspice and nutmeg. Mix well. Stir together the anchovy paste, tomatoes with their juice and fish stock or water. Add to the pot. Bring to a boil, stirring occasionally. Cut the sausage into chunks and return it to the pot.

Cover tightly and simmer over a low heat for 20-40 minutes or until the liquid has been absorbed and the rice is tender.

Meanwhile, cut open the lobster tails and remove the meat. Chop it. Crack the claws.

Add the lobster meat and claws, shrimp and oysters to the jambalaya. Cover and cook for 5 minutes longer.

NOTE: Uncooked shrimp may be used; add them 10 minutes before the lobster and oysters.

SERVES 4-6

Chicken and Sausage Jambalaya.

PORK AND RIB JAMBALAYA

1-1½ lb meaty pork spareribs, cut into
    1-rib pieces
¼ lb bacon
1 onion, peeled and chopped
1-2 garlic cloves, peeled and minced
½ green pepper, cored, seeded and chopped
½ sweet red pepper, cored, seeded and
    chopped
1 celery stalk, chopped
1 eggplant, peeled and chopped
1 cup diced smoked ham
1 lb smoked sausage links, cut into chunks
1½ cups long-grain rice
½ teaspoon mild chili powder
½ teaspoon salt
½ teaspoon black pepper
⅛-¼ teaspoon cayenne
3 cups chicken stock or water

Preheat the oven to 425°.

Arrange the ribs in a greased roasting pan in one layer and bake for 30 minutes.

Meanwhile, fry the bacon in a heavy, large, wide casserole until crisp and rendered of fat. Remove the bacon; drain on paper towels and crumble.

Add the onion, garlic, sweet peppers, celery and eggplant to the bacon fat in the casserole and cook until softened. Add the ham and sausage. Cover and cook 10 minutes, stirring occasionally.

Stir in the rice with the chili powder, salt, pepper and cayenne to taste. Mix in the bacon, then add the stock or water and bring to a boil.

Drain the ribs on paper towels, then bury in the jambalaya. Cover and cook over a low heat for 20-25 minutes or until the rice is tender and all the liquid has been absorbed.

SERVES 6-8

CHICKEN AND SAUSAGE JAMBALAYA

2 tablespoons butter
1 tablespoon corn oil
3-lb chicken, cut into 12 pieces (2 wings, 2
    thighs, 2 drumsticks, 4 breast pieces, 2
    back pieces)
1 cup chopped onions
½ cup chopped scallions
2 garlic cloves, peeled and minced
1 cup chopped green pepper
½ cup chopped celery
½ lb lean boneless pork, cut into small cubes
2 teaspoons salt
½-¾ teaspoon black pepper
¼-½ teaspoon cayenne
½ teaspoon mild chili powder
2 bay leaves
½ teaspoon dried thyme
2 tablespoons chopped fresh parsley
⅛ teaspoon apple pie spice
½ lb spiced or garlic sausage, cut into ½-inch
    thick slices
1 cup diced smoked ham
1 cup long-grain rice
16-oz can whole peeled tomatoes in tomato
    juice
½ cup tomato purée

Melt the butter with the oil in a shallow flameproof casserole and brown the chicken pieces briskly on all sides. Remove the chicken and set aside.

Add the onions, scallions, garlic, green pepper, celery and pork to the casserole and cook about 15 minutes or until the vegetables are softened and golden brown. Stir occasionally to prevent sticking.

Stir in the salt, pepper and cayenne to taste, chili powder, bay leaves, thyme, parsley and spice. Add the sausage, rice, ham, tomatoes with their juice, tomato purée and 2 cups of water. Stir to mix, then bury the chicken pieces in the mixture.

Bring to a boil, then cover and simmer gently for 30 minutes, stirring from time to time. Uncover the casserole and cook for 15 minutes longer. Serve hot.

NOTE: If preferred, the jambalaya may be cooked, covered, in a 350° oven for 1 hour.

SERVES 4-6

VEGETABLES

GRATIN DE POMMES DE TERRE ET ARTICHAUTS

2 lb floury potatoes, peeled
1 large onion, peeled and thinly sliced
16-oz can artichoke hearts in brine, drained and thinly sliced
4 tablespoons butter
1 cup grated Swiss or Gruyère cheese
salt and white pepper
1 cup heavy cream (or half milk and half cream)
Tabasco or other hot pepper sauce

Preheat the oven to 350°.

Parboil the potatoes for 5 minutes, then drain. When cool enough to handle, slice them. Put the onion into a pan of cold water, bring to a boil and blanch for 1 minute; drain.

Layer the potatoes, onion and artichokes in a buttered oval baking dish, measuring about 12×8 inches. Dot each layer with a little butter, sprinkle with a little cheese and season to taste with salt and pepper. Finish with a layer of potatoes, sprinkled with the remaining cheese and dotted with the rest of the butter.

Scald the cream and stir in Tabasco to taste. Pour over the potato mixture. Bake for 1 hour or until the potatoes are tender and the top of the gratin is golden brown. Serve hot.

SERVES 6-8

PEPPERED PEAS

1½ cups shelled fresh peas
1 cup shredded lettuce
⅓ cup chopped scallions
½ cup diced sweet red pepper
1 large ripe, flavorsome tomato, diced
1 teaspoon sugar
salt and black pepper
½ lb zucchini, diced
1-2 tablespoons butter

Put the peas, lettuce, scallions, red pepper, tomato, sugar, and salt and pepper to taste in a saucepan. Half cover and cook gently for 15 minutes, stirring occasionally.

Add the zucchini and cook uncovered for a further 5 minutes or until the vegetables are tender.

Add the butter and stir in until melted. Serve hot.

NOTE: If fresh peas are not available, frozen may be used. Add them with the zucchini.

SALADE VERTE

1 cup green beans cut into ¾-inch pieces
½ cup frozen peas
1 cup zucchini cut into ¾-inch sticks
¼ cup diced celery
¼ cup diced green pepper
¼ cup finely chopped scallions
6 tablespoons salad or olive oil
2½ tablespoons lemon juice
½ teaspoon sugar
¼ teaspoon mustard powder
⅛ teaspoon hot paprika
salt and white pepper
Tabasco or other hot pepper sauce

Drop the green beans into a pan of boiling water. Bring back to a boil and simmer 2 minutes. Add the peas and simmer 2 minutes longer. Add the zucchini and continue simmering for 1 minute. Drain the vegetables, rinse in cold water to stop the cooking and drain well again.

Put the cooked vegetables in a mixing bowl and add the celery, green pepper and scallions.

In another bowl, or a screwtop jar, combine the oil, lemon juice, sugar, mustard powder, paprika, and salt, pepper and Tabasco to taste. Mix well.

Add the dressing to the vegetables and toss together. Serve at cool room temperature.

Peppered Peas (top), Salade Verte (bottom).

LÉGUMES VERTS GRATINÉS

2 10-oz packages frozen chopped spinach
2 tablespoons butter
1 small onion, peeled and finely chopped
8 oz cream cheese, at room temperature
1 cup light cream or milk
1 large egg, beaten
¼ teaspoon grated nutmeg
salt and black pepper
Tabasco or other hot pepper sauce
16-oz can artichoke hearts in brine, drained
    and sliced
½ canned pimiento, cut into strips
⅓ cup freshly grated Parmesan cheese
⅓ cup fine bread crumbs, preferably from
    day-old French bread

Thaw and cook the spinach according to the directions on the package. Drain well. When cool enough to handle, squeeze the spinach to remove all excess liquid. Put into a mixing bowl.

Preheat the oven to 350°.

Melt the butter in a small pan and cook the onion until softened. Add to the spinach, with the cream cheese, cream or milk, egg, nutmeg, and salt, pepper and Tabasco to taste. Mix well together.

Spread out half the spinach mixture in a layer in a buttered baking dish. Cover with the artichoke hearts and pimiento, then top with the remaining spinach mixture. Mix together the Parmesan cheese and crumbs and sprinkle over the top.

Bake for 30-40 minutes or until lightly puffed up and set and the top is golden brown. Serve hot.

SERVES 6

HOT POTATO SALAD

2 lb small new potatoes, preferably
    red-skinned
¼ lb sliced bacon
1 large egg
3 tablespoons medium dry white wine
3 tablespoons cider vinegar
1½ teaspoons sugar
¼ teaspoon dried hot red pepper flakes
salt and black pepper
½ cup chopped scallions
3 tablespoons chopped fresh parsley

Cook the potatoes in boiling water until just tender. Drain well. When cool enough to handle, peel the potatoes if desired and cut them into thick slices. Keep hot.

Cook the bacon in a skillet until crisp and browned. Drain the bacon on paper towels, then crumble. Set aside.

Pour off all but 3 tablespoons bacon fat from the skillet. Lightly beat the egg with the wine, vinegar, sugar, pepper flakes, and salt and pepper to taste. Add to the bacon fat in the skillet and cook very gently until just thickened, whisking constantly.

Add the dressing to the potatoes with the scallions and toss gently. Sprinkle the bacon and parsley on top and serve.

YAMS À LA MAISON

2½-3 lb orange-fleshed sweet potatoes
    (yams)
7-8 oz cream cheese
1 egg
1 teaspoon ground cinnamon
¼ teaspoon ground coriander
¼ teaspoon grated nutmeg
salt and black pepper
½ cup peach, apricot or pineapple preserves
½ cup coarsely chopped pecans or walnuts

Preheat the oven to 375°.

Scrub the potatoes and prick them in several places. Bake, on a baking sheet, for 1-1½ hours or until tender.

When cool enough to handle, peel the potatoes and put them into a mixing bowl. Add the cream cheese, egg, spices, and salt and pepper to taste. Whip with an electric beater until smooth and fluffy. Spoon into a buttered baking dish and smooth over the top.

Warm the preserves until melted, then stir in the nuts. Spread over the potato mixture. Bake 20 minutes, and serve hot.

SERVES 6

POIVRONS FARCIS

2 sweet red peppers
2 green peppers
2 bacon slices, chopped
1 small onion, peeled and finely chopped
1 garlic clove, peeled and minced
1 cup long-grain rice
1 cup diced mushrooms
½ cup fresh corn kernels
1½ cups chicken stock or water
¼ cup chopped fresh parsley
2 tablespoons chopped fresh chives or green
* scallion tops*
1 tablespoon chopped fresh thyme, or
* 1 teaspoon dried thyme*
salt and black pepper
1 large egg
¼ cup light cream or milk

Trim the stems off the peppers. Cut them in half lengthwise and cut out the white ribs. Rinse out the seeds. Blanch the pepper halves in boiling water for 4 minutes. Drain and set aside.

Fry the bacon with the onion and garlic in a saucepan until golden brown. Add the rice, mushrooms and corn and cook, stirring, for 1 minute. Add the stock or water. Bring to a boil, stir once, then cover and simmer gently for 15-20 minutes or until the rice is tender and all the liquid has been absorbed.

Preheat the oven to 350°.

Add the herbs and salt and pepper to taste to the rice mixture. Lightly beat the egg with the cream or milk and stir in thoroughly.

Stuff the pepper halves with the rice mixture and arrange them in an oiled baking dish. Bake for 30 minutes. Serve hot or cold.

Hot Potato Salad.

BAKED CUSHAW

1 large cushaw (2-3 lb)
5 tablespoons butter
⅓ cup granulated sugar
1 teaspoon salt
¼ teaspoon black pepper
½ teaspoon ground cinnamon
¼ teaspoon ground cloves or allspice
¼ teaspoon grated nutmeg
2 tablespoons light brown sugar

Peel the cushaw, cut it in half and scoop out the seeds. Cut the squash into 1 inch cubes and put them in a heavy saucepan with ⅓ cup water. Bring to a boil, then cover and cook for 5-10 minutes or until tender. Uncover and boil away the excess water. Add 4 tablespoons of the butter and the granulated sugar and cook until golden brown and beginning to caramelize. Stir frequently as the mixture will tend to stick to the pan. Stir in the salt, pepper and spices.

Preheat the oven to 400°.

Tip the squash mixture into a buttered baking dish. Sprinkle over the brown sugar and dot with the remaining butter. Bake about 40 minutes or until the top is crisp and browned.

NOTE: A cushaw is a squash that looks like a giant zucchini.

SERVES 6

POTATOES BAKED WITH GARLIC BUTTER

2 lb new potatoes, preferably red-skinned,
    well scrubbed
6 tablespoons butter
2-3 garlic cloves, peeled and minced
1-2 teaspoons salt
½ teaspoon black pepper
¼ teaspoon white pepper
¼-½ teaspoon cayenne

Preheat the oven to 375°.

Cook the potatoes in boiling water for 10-15 minutes or until they are almost tender. Drain well. When cool enough to handle, peel them if desired, and cut into ½ inch cubes. Put them into a baking dish.

Melt the butter in a small saucepan and add the garlic. Cook until the garlic starts to turn golden, swirling the butter around in the pan. For a less strong garlic flavor, strain the butter over the potatoes and discard the garlic in the strainer. Alternatively, pour the garlic and butter over the potatoes. Sprinkle over the seasonings. Toss to coat the potato pieces evenly.

Bake for 25-30 minutes or until tender and golden brown.

CORN WITH SPICED BUTTER

4-6 tablespoons butter, at room temperature
½ teaspoon salt
¼ teaspoon black pepper
⅛ teaspoon cayenne
⅛ teaspoon Tabasco or other hot pepper
    sauce
2-3 drops Angostura bitters
4 ears fresh corn, shucked
1 teaspoon sugar

Beat the butter with the salt, pepper, cayenne, Tabasco and bitters. Spread it out about ¼ inch thick on a piece of foil. Cover and refrigerate until firm.

Drop the corn into a large pan of boiling water to which the sugar has been added. Bring back to a boil and simmer 4-7 minutes, depending on the size and age of the ears.

Cut the spiced butter into four portions, using a decorative cutter if desired.

Drain the corn and serve with the spiced butter.

NOTE: The spiced butter is also delicious used to dress other hot freshly cooked vegetables, such as green beans, peas, zucchini and potatoes.

MAQUE CHOUX

4 large ears fresh corn, shucked
3 tablespoons bacon fat or butter
1 onion, peeled and finely chopped
½ cup chopped tomato (peeled if necessary)
½ tablespoon sugar
¼ teaspoon salt
¼ teaspoon white pepper
⅛ - ¼ teaspoon cayenne

Cut the kernels from the ears of corn, then scrape the cobs with the back of a knife to extract the milky liquid. There should be about 1½-2 cups of kernels.

Melt the bacon fat or butter in a heavy saucepan and add the corn kernels and milky liquid, onion, tomato, sugar, salt, pepper and cayenne to taste. Stir to mix, then cover and cook over a gentle heat for 45 minutes, stirring occasionally.

MIRLITONS PONTCHARTRAIN

4 large mirlitons (chayotes)
4 tablespoons butter
½ cup chopped scallions
1 garlic clove, peeled and minced
1 cup chopped mushrooms
1½ cups chopped cooked shrimp
1½ cups fresh bread crumbs, preferably from
    day-old French bread
⅓ cup heavy or light cream
salt and white pepper
Tabasco or other hot pepper sauce
2 tablespoons chopped fresh parsley

Preheat the oven to 350°.

Cook the mirlitons whole in boiling water until tender, 45 minutes to 1 hour. Drain. When cool enough to handle, halve them lengthwise and discard the seed, if any. Scoop out the flesh, leaving shells about ¼ inch thick. Set the shells aside. Finely chop the flesh and drain well in a strainer.

Heat 2 tablespoons of the butter in a small skillet and cook the scallions, garlic and mushrooms until softened, 2-3 minutes. Remove from the heat and mix in the mirliton flesh, shrimp, 1 cup of the crumbs mixed with the cream, and salt, pepper and Tabasco to taste. Stuff the mirliton shells with the mixture and arrange side by side in a buttered baking dish.

Melt the remaining butter in a small saucepan and stir in the parsley and remaining crumbs. Sprinkle this mixture over the stuffing. Bake 20-30 minutes or until golden brown on top. Serve hot.

STUFFED ZUCCHINI RINGS

4 large, fat, straight zucchini
2 tablespoons olive oil
1 small onion, peeled and finely chopped
1 garlic clove, peeled and minced
1 small celery stalk, diced
½ green pepper, cored, seeded and diced
½ lb bulk pork sausage
1 cup fresh bread crumbs, preferably from
    day-old French bread
1 large egg, beaten
2 teaspoons Pickapeppa sauce
½ teaspoon dried thyme
pinch of dried hot red pepper flakes
salt and black pepper
oil for brushing

Preheat the oven to 375°.

Trim off the ends of the zucchini and cut them in half crosswise. Using an apple corer, hollow out the center seeds and pulp, leaving a zucchini shell about ¼ inch thick and making a hole all the way through for the stuffing. Set the zucchini shells aside and finely chop the pulp and seeds.

Heat the olive oil in a small skillet and cook the onion, garlic, celery, green pepper and zucchini pulp until softened and excess liquid has evaporated. Tip the vegetable mixture into a bowl and add the pork sausage, bread crumbs, egg, Pickapeppa sauce, thyme, pepper flakes, and salt and pepper to taste. Mix together thoroughly with the hands.

Stuff the zucchini shells with the sausage mixture. Spread the remaining sausage mixture over the bottom of a greased baking dish. Arrange the stuffed zucchini on top and brush them with a little oil. Bake for 30 minutes or until the zucchini are just tender and the stuffing is browned. Serve hot, cut into slices crosswise.

CRAB-STUFFED EGGPLANT ROLLS

2 large eggplants
2-3 tablespoons olive oil
1 onion, peeled and finely chopped
1 garlic clove, peeled and minced
½ sweet red pepper, cored, seeded and finely
    chopped
16-oz can chopped tomatoes in tomato juice
½ tablespoon tomato paste
1 teaspoon Worcestershire sauce
½ teaspoon sugar
salt and black pepper
cayenne
1 cup flaked white crabmeat
½ teaspoon finely grated lemon rind
½ cup fresh bread crumbs, preferably from
    French bread
2-3 tablespoons freshly grated Parmesan
    cheese

Preheat the oven to 400°.

Cut the eggplants lengthwise into eight center slices, each about ¼ inch thick. Brush on both sides with oil and arrange on a baking sheet. Bake for 5-10 minutes or until bendable.

Meanwhile, heat 1 tablespoon oil in a saucepan and cook the onion, garlic and sweet pepper until softened. Add the tomatoes with their juice, the tomato paste, Worcestershire sauce, sugar, and salt, pepper and cayenne to taste and stir well. Bring to a boil, then simmer for 20 minutes, stirring occasionally.

Purée the sauce in a blender or food processor. Pour ½ cup sauce into a mixing bowl and add the crabmeat, lemon rind and crumbs. Mix well. Spread this mixture evenly over the eggplant slices and roll them up. Pack the rolls into an oiled baking dish and pour over the remaining tomato sauce. Sprinkle the cheese on top.

Bake at 350° for 20-30 minutes or until the top is golden brown and the rolls are piping hot.

SERVES 6-8

BAYOU RATATOUILLE

2 tablespoons olive oil
1 large onion, peeled and chopped
1-2 garlic cloves, peeled and minced
½ lb baby okra, trimmed and halved
    lengthwise
1 small eggplant, cut into chunks
½ lb zucchini, thickly sliced
½ green pepper, cored, seeded and cut into
    strips
½ sweet red pepper, cored, seeded and cut
    into strips
16-oz can peeled whole tomatoes in tomato
    juice
1 tablespoon tomato paste
1 tablespoon red wine vinegar
½ teaspoon sugar
salt and black pepper
Tabasco or other hot pepper sauce

Heat the oil in a heavy saucepan and cook the onion and garlic until softened, stirring occasionally. Add the okra and cook gently for 10 minutes, stirring from time to time.

Add the remaining ingredients, with salt, pepper and Tabasco to taste. Stir well to mix, then cover and cook for 30-40 minutes or until all the vegetables are tender. Stir occasionally during cooking.

Serve hot or cold.

SERVES 6-8

Bayou Ratatouille.

NEW ORLEANS-STYLE ARTICHOKES

4 globe artichokes
juice of ½ lemon
1 bay leaf
few black peppercorns
1 cup diced cooked ham
1 cup diced garlic sausage
½ cup chopped scallions
1 garlic clove, peeled and minced (optional)
⅓ cup diced green pepper
⅓ cup diced sweet red pepper
⅓ cup diced celery
2 tablespoons chopped fresh parsley
Dressing:
¾ cup olive oil
6 tablespoons lemon juice
1 tablespoon Dijon mustard
2 teaspoons sugar
1 teaspoon salt
½ teaspoon white pepper
Tabasco or other hot pepper sauce

Trim the stalks of the artichokes level with the base. Cut off the top one-third of the leaves, then trim the pointed tips off the side leaves. Drop the artichokes into a large saucepan of boiling water to which the lemon juice, bay leaf and peppercorns have been added. Simmer for 20-30 minutes or until tender. To test if an artichoke is done, tug at a leaf: it should come away with little resistance. Drain the artichokes, then leave to drain completely and cool upside-down.

Meanwhile, combine all the dressing ingredients in a mixing bowl and lightly mix together with a wire whisk. Add Tabasco sauce to taste.

Transfer half the dressing to another bowl. Add the ham, sausage, scallions, garlic, sweet peppers, celery and parsley and stir to mix. Cover and leave to marinate until ready to serve.

When the artichokes have cooled, open up the tops and remove the small center leaves and the hairy choke. Be sure to remove all the choke as it is inedible.

Spoon the ham mixture into the artichokes and stand each one on a plate (preferably a special artichoke plate that has plenty of room for the discarded leaves). Drizzle the remaining dressing down around the outside leaves, and serve.

BAKING

SPICED BANANA MUFFINS

4 tablespoons butter
½ cup sugar
¾ cup ripe banana mashed with 1 teaspoon
    lemon juice
1 large egg, beaten
1¼ cups all-purpose flour
½ tablespoon baking powder
¼ teaspoon ground allspice
⅛ teaspoon grated nutmeg
pinch of salt
½ cup milk
1 teaspoon vanilla

Preheat the oven to 375°.

Beat the butter and sugar together until light and fluffy. Beat in the banana and egg. Sift in the flour, baking powder, spices and salt. Add the milk and vanilla and mix well together.

Divide between 12-14 greased muffin tins. Bake about 20-25 minutes or until puffed up and golden brown. Serve warm or cold.

MAKES 12-14

HOT AND SPICY CRACKLIN' BREAD

¾ cup all-purpose flour
¾ cup yellow cornmeal
2 teaspoons baking powder
½ teaspoon salt
½ teaspoon black pepper
¼ teaspoon cayenne
1½ cups milk or water
1 tablespoon bacon fat or butter
¼ teaspoon Tabasco or other hot pepper
    sauce
½ cup broken cracklin' or crumbled
    crisp-fried bacon
oil for deep frying

Sift the flour, cornmeal, baking powder, salt, pepper and cayenne into a mixing bowl.

Heat the milk or water with the bacon fat or butter and Tabasco until bubbles appear around the edge. Add to the dry ingredients and stir together. Stir in the cracklin' or bacon.

Drop heaped tablespoonfuls of the batter into oil heated to 375° and deep fry until dark golden brown. Drain on paper towels and serve hot.

SERVES 6-8

COUCH-COUCH

2 cups yellow cornmeal
1 teaspoon salt
1 teaspoon baking powder
1 tablespoon sugar
1½ cups milk or water
⅓ cup corn oil

Mix together the cornmeal, salt, baking powder, sugar and milk or water to make a batter.

Heat the oil in a heavy skillet, pour in the batter and cook until a golden brown crust forms on the bottom. Stir well to break up the crust and mix it into the still liquid batter, then reduce the heat to very low and cover the pan. Cook about 15 minutes, stirring often, until golden brown and crumbly.

Serve hot, as a cereal with milk and sugar, or with bacon and cane syrup.

VARIATION: Omit the sugar, if desired, and deep fry spoonfuls of the batter in oil heated to 375° until golden brown. Drain these fritters on paper towels and serve hot.

HONEY YAM BISCUITS

2 cups all-purpose flour
1 tablespoon baking powder
1 teaspoon salt
1 teaspoon ground ginger
¼ teaspoon grated nutmeg
¾ cup puréed orange-fleshed sweet potato
   (yam), preferably freshly cooked
4 tablespoons butter, melted
2-3 tablespoons honey
⅓-½ cup light cream

Preheat the oven to 425°.
   Sift the flour, baking powder, salt, ginger and nutmeg into a mixing bowl. Add the sweet potato purée, butter and honey and mix well. Gradually mix in enough cream to make a soft dough.
   Roll out the dough on a lightly floured surface to about ¾-inch thick. Cut out 2 inch rounds and place on an ungreased baking sheet.
   Bake for 15-20 minutes or until risen and lightly golden. Serve warm.

MAKES ABOUT 16

PAIN PERDU

2 large eggs
¾ cup milk
1 tablespoon sugar (optional)
¼-½ teaspoon vanilla
24 slices of stale French bread, cut on a slant
6-8 tablespoons butter, at room temperature
2 tablespoons honey
butter for frying

Lightly beat the eggs with the milk, sugar (if using) and vanilla in a wide shallow dish. Add the bread slices, turning them to coat both sides. Leave to soak while making the honey butter.
   Beat the butter with the honey until smoothly combined.
   Heat a little butter in a heavy skillet and fry the bread slices, in batches, until golden brown on both sides. Add more butter to the skillet as necessary.
   Serve the bread hot with the honey butter.

HUSH PUPPIES

1 cup yellow cornmeal
1 teaspoon baking powder
2 teaspoons sugar
½ teaspoon salt
¼ teaspoon black pepper
1 egg
½ cup buttermilk or milk
¼ cup chopped scallions
oil for deep frying

Sift the cornmeal, baking powder, sugar, salt and pepper into a mixing bowl. Add the egg and buttermilk or milk and mix well. Stir in the scallions.
   Drop heaped tablespoonfuls of the batter into oil heated to 375° and deep fry until dark golden brown. Drain on paper towels and serve hot.

SERVES 4-6

ORANGE PECAN MUFFINS

1 stick butter, at room temperature
1 cup light brown sugar
¾ teaspoon grated orange rind
2 large eggs
2 cups all-purpose flour
1½ teaspoons baking powder
½ cup milk
½ cup orange juice
½ cup coarsely chopped pecans
sifted confectioners' sugar (optional)

Preheat the oven to 350°.

Beat the butter with the sugar and orange rind until creamy and well mixed. Beat in the eggs, followed by the flour and baking powder. Beat in the milk and orange juice. Stir in the pecans.

Spoon into buttered muffin tins. Bake for 20-25 minutes or until puffed and golden brown. Cool in the tins for 5 minutes, then turn out and cool completely on a wire rack.

Sprinkle the tops with a little confectioners' sugar, if desired.

MAKES ABOUT 16

DEVILED HAM BISCUITS

3 cups all-purpose flour
1 teaspoon salt
1½-2 teaspoons mustard powder
¼-½ teaspoon cayenne
1½ tablespoons baking powder
3 tablespoons butter
½ cup ground smoked ham
1¼-1½ cups buttermilk

Preheat the oven to 400°.

Sift the flour, salt, mustard powder, cayenne and baking powder into a mixing bowl. Cut and rub in the butter until resembling fine crumbs. Mix in the ham. Bind to a soft dough with the buttermilk.

Roll out the dough on a lightly floured surface to about ¾-inch thick. Cut out 2-inch rounds and place them on an ungreased baking sheet. Bake about 15 minutes or until puffed up and golden brown. Serve warm.

MAKES 24

Honey Yam Biscuits (left);
Orange Pecan Muffins (right).

DESSERTS

BANANAS FOSTER

4 tablespoons butter
½ cup light brown sugar
½ teaspoon ground cinnamon
6 tablespoons banana liqueur or brandy
4 large bananas, halved lengthwise and then
    crosswise
6 tablespoons rum
4 scoops vanilla ice cream

Melt the butter in a skillet or chafing dish. Add the sugar, cinnamon and banana liqueur or brandy and stir to dissolve the sugar. Bring to a boil. Add the bananas and cook until just soft and lightly browned, turning occasionally.

Warm the rum in a small saucepan and pour over the bananas. Set alight. Carefully tilt the pan to swirl the liquid around until the flames die out.

Divide the bananas between four plates. Top each serving with a scoop of ice cream and spoon the sauce over. Serve immediately.

PECAN TASSIES

3 oz cream cheese, at room temperature
1 stick butter, at room temperature
1 cup all-purpose flour
1 large egg
1 large egg yolk
1 cup firmly packed dark brown sugar
pinch of salt
1 teaspoon vanilla
1 tablespoon bourbon
1 cup coarsely broken pecans

Combine the cream cheese, butter and flour in a mixing bowl and work to a smooth dough. Alternatively, do this in a food processor. Wrap and chill for 30 minutes.

Preheat the oven to 350°.

Divide the dough into 24 equal portions and shape into balls.

Combine the egg, egg yolk, sugar, salt, vanilla and bourbon in a mixing bowl and beat well until smooth and creamy. Stir in the pecans.

Line 2-inch diameter muffin tins with the dough, pressing it over the bottoms and about two-thirds of the way up the sides. Spoon the filling into the pastry cases; do not fill above the level of the dough.

Bake for 20 minutes or until the pastry is golden brown and the filling is puffed up. Cool in the tins for 10 minutes before transferring to wire racks to cool completely.

MAKES 24

CREOLE KISSES

2 large egg whites
½ cup sugar
⅛-¼ teaspoon sweet orange oil, or orange
    extract to taste
1 cup finely ground pecans, or half pecans
    and half almonds

Preheat the oven to 350°.

Beat the egg whites until foamy. Add 2 tablespoons of the sugar and the orange oil or extract and continue beating until stiff and glossy. Fold in the remaining sugar with the nuts.

Line baking sheets with edible rice paper or parchment paper. Drop the batter from a teaspoon onto the paper, leaving room for each cookie to spread out.

Bake for 10-12 minutes or until just tinged brown around the edges and firm to a gentle touch. Cool on the baking sheets before removing from the parchment paper, or tearing the rice paper around each cookie.

MAKES ABOUT 24

Bananas Foster.

AMBROSIA

4-6 large seedless oranges
1 cup grated fresh coconut
2-3 tablespoons Cointreau
1 tablespoon lemon juice
⅓-½ cup confectioners' sugar, sifted

Peel the oranges and slice them thinly. Do this over a bowl to catch all the juice.

Layer the oranges and coconut in a serving dish, sprinkling each layer with the Cointreau, lemon juice and sugar. Add any orange juice.

Cover and chill for 1-2 hours before serving.

VARIATION: If fresh coconut is not available, shredded dried coconut may be used instead. If desired, toast the coconut under the broiler.

LES OREILLES DES COCHONS

2 cups all-purpose flour
½ teaspoon baking powder
pinch of salt
4 tablespoons butter
2 large eggs, beaten
1 teaspoon vinegar
oil for deep frying
sifted confectioners' sugar

Sift the flour, baking powder and salt into a bowl. Cut and rub in the butter until resembling fine crumbs, then add the eggs and vinegar and bind to a dough. Add a few drops of water if necessary.

Divide the dough into about 32 portions and shape each into a ball. Roll out each ball very thinly – ⅛-inch or less – to a round 3-4 inches in diameter. Using the end of a wooden spoon, push into the center from one side of a round; this will result in the traditional pig's ear shape.

Deep fry in oil heated to 360° for 2-3 minutes or until golden brown on both sides. Drain on paper towels.

Dredge with confectioners' sugar before serving. These are particularly delicious served warm.

VARIATION: Instead of confectioners' sugar, the cookies may be coated with a caramel syrup (sugar and water boiled to 238°) and sprinkled with chopped pecans.

MAKES ABOUT 32

ICED CAFÉ BRÛLOT

½ cup sugar
2 cups warm strong chicory coffee
4 tablespoons Cognac
1 tablespoon Cointreau
2 egg whites
ground cinnamon (optional)

Dissolve the sugar in the coffee. Stir in the Cognac and Cointreau and cool. Pour into ice cube trays, with dividers, and freeze about 2 hours or until just set.

Beat the egg whites until stiff.

Tip the coffee ice cubes into a blender or food processor and whirl to a slush. Tip into a bowl and fold in the egg whites. Work quickly so the coffee ice cubes do not melt. Return to the ice cube trays (without the dividers) and freeze again until firm.

For serving, allow to soften at room temperature only as long as it takes to become spoonable (or scoopable). If desired, sprinkle each serving with a little cinnamon.

SERVES 6

FRENCH APPLE PIE

1 cup all-purpose flour
pinch of salt
2 tablespoons + 1 teaspoon sugar
6 tablespoons butter or margarine
2-3 tablespoons ice water
¼ lb frozen puff pastry, thawed
1-2 tablespoons heavy cream
Filling:
2 lb crisp, tart apples, peeled, cored and
    sliced (about 4 cups)
2 tablespoons all-purpose flour
½ cup sugar
1 teaspoon ground cinnamon
¼ teaspoon ground allspice
¼ teaspoon ground coriander
½ cup heavy cream
2 tablespoons apple brandy or Calvados
2 tablespoons butter

Ambrosia.

Preheat the oven to 325°.

Sift the flour, salt and 1 teaspoon sugar into a mixing bowl. Cut and rub in the butter or margarine until resembling fine crumbs, then bind to a dough with ice water. Chill while making the filling.

Put the apples in a mixing bowl. Sprinkle over the flour, sugar and spices and toss to coat the apples evenly.

Roll out the dough on a lightly floured surface and use to line an 8½-inch pie pan. Tip the apple mixture into the piecrust. Pour over the cream mixed with the brandy and dot the top with the butter.

Roll out the puff pastry on a lightly floured surface and cut into thin strips. Lay these over the apples to make a lattice and seal firmly to the piecrust edge with a little water. Brush the pastry strips with the cream and sprinkle with the remaining 2 tablespoons sugar.

Bake for 1 hour or until the apples are tender and the pastry is golden brown. Serve warm.

NOTE: Choose a variety of apple that will keep its shape during cooking.

SERVES 6-8

LAYERED HAZELNUT TORTE

6 large eggs, separated
1½ cups sugar
¼ cup self-rising cake flour
1½ cups ground hazelnuts
sifted confectioners' sugar to decorate
Buttercream filling:
1 stick unsalted butter, at room temperature
scant 1 cup confectioners' sugar, sifted
1 teaspoon vanilla

Preheat the oven to 350°.

Beat the egg yolks with the sugar until pale and thick. Beat in the flour (the mixture will be very thick).

In another bowl, beat the egg whites until stiff. Add a large spoonful of the whites to the egg yolk mixture and beat in gently to soften it. Fold in the nuts, then fold in the remaining egg whites.

Divide the batter between two buttered and floured (or parchment paper lined) layer cake pans that measure about 8½ inches across the base. Bake for 25-30 minutes or until risen and golden brown and just firm to the touch in the center. Cool in the pans, placed on a wire rack.

To make the buttercream, beat the butter with the sugar and vanilla until evenly mixed and smooth.

Remove the cake layers from the pans. Place one layer on a serving plate and cover with the buttercream. Place the other layer on top. Sprinkle the top with confectioners' sugar.

NOTE: For a special occasion, top the cake with small, well-drained strawberries, raspberries or other berries just before serving. The cake can be filled with sweetened, vanilla-flavored whipped cream instead of buttercream, if preferred.

SERVES 6-8

SPICED PEACH TART

2 cups all-purpose flour
½ cup finely chopped pecans
½ teaspoon salt
⅓ cup sugar
10 tablespoons (1¼ sticks) butter
1 egg, beaten
½ teaspoon vanilla
Filling:
2 lb ripe peaches, peeled, pitted and sliced
juice of 1 lemon
3 tablespoons all-purpose flour
¼ cup sugar
¼ teaspoon ground cinnamon

Mix together the flour, pecans, salt and sugar in a mixing bowl. Cut in the butter, then rub in with the fingertips until the mixture resembles fine crumbs. Add the egg and vanilla and bind to a dough. Wrap and chill for 30 minutes.

Preheat the oven to 400°.

The dough is very rich and crumbly, so roll it out between sheets of plastic wrap or wax paper. Alternatively, just press it out in the mold. Use the dough to line an 11½-inch diameter porcelain or ceramic fluted quiche mold. Prick all over with a fork (or line with parchment paper and weigh down with baking beans). Bake unfilled for 10 minutes.

Toss the peach slices with the lemon juice.

Mix together the flour, sugar and cinnamon and sprinkle over the bottom of the pastry case. Arrange the peach slices in the case. Bake for 25 minutes.

Dip a pastry brush in the syrup that will have formed around the peaches and use this to glaze the top slices. Bake for 10 minutes longer or until the pastry is set and golden brown. Serve warm or cold.

NOTE: Any leftover pastry dough is delicious baked as cookies. Shape the dough into walnut-sized balls and arrange on a lightly greased cookie sheet. Flatten each ball slightly with the tines of a fork. Bake about 25-30 minutes or until set and lightly browned.

Layered Hazelnut Torte (left); Spiced Peach Tart (right).

ICED AMARETTO MOUSSES

3 large eggs, separated
⅓ cup sugar
3 tablespoons Amaretto di Saronno liqueur
1 cup heavy cream
toasted sliced almonds for decoration

Combine the egg yolks, sugar and Amaretto in a large mixing bowl. Beat with an electric mixer until very thick and light in color, and at least doubled in volume.

Whip the cream until thick. Beat the egg whites until stiff. Fold the cream into the Amaretto mixture, and then fold in the egg whites.

Divide the mixture between 8 ramekins or other small serving dishes (they must be freezerproof). Cover and freeze for about 4 hours or until firm.

Allow the mousses to soften at room temperature for 5-10 minutes, then sprinkle toasted sliced almonds on top and serve.

SERVES 8

SWEET POTATO PIE

1 cup all-purpose flour
pinch of salt
5 tablespoons butter or margarine
2-3 tablespoons ice water
Filling:
1½ cups puréed orange-fleshed sweet
  potatoes (yams), preferably freshly cooked
½ cup firmly packed light brown sugar
2 large eggs, beaten
1 cup light cream
4-6 tablespoons Southern Comfort
1½ teaspoons finely grated orange rind
⅛ teaspoon salt
¾ teaspoon ground cinnamon
¼ teaspoon ground allspice
⅛ teaspoon grated nutmeg

Sift the flour and salt into a mixing bowl. Cut and rub in the butter or margarine until resembling fine crumbs, then bind to a dough with ice water. Cover and chill while making the filling.

Combine all the filling ingredients in a mixing bowl and beat lightly but thoroughly together.

Preheat the oven to 350°.

Roll out the dough on a lightly floured surface and use to line an 8½-inch pie pan. Pour the filling into the pie crust. Bake for 45-50 minutes or until just set. Serve warm or cold.

NOTE: Canned sweet potatoes (yams) may be used, but drain them well before mashing or puréeing in a blender or food processor.

SERVES 6-8

Iced Amaretto Mousses.

SAZERAC CREAM PIE

1¼ cups finely crushed graham crackers
4 tablespoons butter, melted
2 cups milk
⅔ cup sugar
3 large eggs
2 tablespoons cornstarch
1 envelope unflavored gelatin, softened in
    2 tablespoons water
4 tablespoons bourbon
¾ teaspoon Pernod or other anise-flavored
    liqueur
10 drops Angostura bitters
1½ cups heavy cream
1 teaspoon grated lemon rind

Mix together the cracker crumbs and melted butter. Set aside 4 heaping tablespoons of the mixture for the topping, and press the remainder over the bottom of a greased 8½-inch pie pan. Refrigerate.

Scald the milk in a heavy saucepan. Meanwhile, lightly beat together the sugar, eggs and cornstarch. Add the hot milk, stirring well, then pour the mixture back into the saucepan. Cook over a gentle heat, stirring constantly, until this custard thickens enough to coat the back of a wooden spoon.

Remove from the heat and stir in the softened gelatin until completely dissolved. Strain the custard into a mixing bowl. Stir in the bourbon, Pernod and bitters. Cool, then chill until thickened to the consistency of unbeaten egg whites.

Whip the cream and whisk lightly into the thickened custard mixture. Pour into the pan over the crumb base. Chill until set.

Mix the reserved crumb mixture with the lemon rind and sprinkle over the top of the pie before serving.

SERVES 6-8

GLACE ABSINTHE

4 egg yolks
½ cup sugar
pinch of salt
1 cup milk
¼ cup absinthe substitute (Pernod or Ricard)
1½ cups heavy cream

Beat the egg yolks, sugar and salt together until very pale and thick.

Meanwhile, heat the milk in a heavy saucepan until scalded (bubbles just begin to appear around the edge). Stir the milk into the egg-yolk mixture, then pour back into the pan. Cook over a very low heat, stirring constantly, until the custard thickens enough to coat the back of the spoon. Cool, stirring occasionally.

Stir the Pernod or Ricard into the custard.

Whip the cream until thick and gently fold into the custard. Pour into a metal container, cover and freeze for 1-2 hours or until slushy.

Tip the slushy ice cream into a mixing bowl and beat to break down the ice crystals. Return to the metal tray and freeze again until firm.

If solidly frozen, after prolonged freezing, allow to soften at room temperature for 10-15 minutes before serving.

SERVES 4-6

STUFFED NECTARINES

3 oz cream cheese
3 tablespoons apricot or peach preserves
4 ripe but firm nectarines, halved and pitted
½ cup Southern Comfort
¼ cup sliced almonds

Preheat the oven to 350°.

Beat together the cream cheese and preserves. Spoon into the hollows in the nectarines and arrange in a buttered baking dish. Pour around the Southern Comfort and sprinkle over the almonds.

Bake for 30 minutes or until the nectarines are hot and the nuts are lightly browned. Serve hot or cold.

Chocolate Bourbon Balls and Pralines.

CHOCOLATE BOURBON BALLS

2 oz semisweet chocolate
1 tablespoon butter
about 4 tablespoons bourbon
1 cup confectioners' sugar, sifted
1½ cups finely crushed vanilla wafers
1 cup coarsely chopped pecans
sifted confectioners' sugar for dredging

Melt the chocolate with the butter and bourbon over a gentle heat, stirring until smooth. Scrape into a mixing bowl and stir in the sugar. Mix in the cookies and then the pecans. If the mixture seems too stiff and dry, add another tablespoon of bourbon.

Shape into walnut-sized balls and coat all over with confectioners' sugar. Store in an airtight container.

MAKES 30-32

PRALINES

1½ cups granulated sugar
1 cup firmly packed light brown sugar
½ cup firmly packed dark brown sugar
pinch of salt
⅔ cup milk
½ cup heavy cream
4 tablespoons butter
1 teaspoon vanilla
1½ cups coarsely broken pecans

Combine the sugars, salt, milk, cream, butter and vanilla in a heavy pan. Stir to dissolve the sugar, then bring to a boil and boil until the mixture will form a soft ball when dropped in cold water or a temperature of 238° if using a sugar thermometer.

Remove from the heat and cool for about 1 minute, then add the pecans and beat with a wooden spoon until the mixture turns creamy. Immediately, drop of small spoonfuls onto buttered foil or wax paper. The mixture will harden as it cools; if this happens before all the pralines are shaped, add 1-2 tablespoons hot water to the mixture still in the pan.

NOTE: Pralines do not keep well, but for maximum storage life wrap them individually and tightly in foil and store in an airtight container.

BOURBON BREAD PUDDING

24 slices stale French bread, each ½-inch
thick
2 cups milk (or half milk and half cream)
1 cinnamon stick, lightly crushed
large strip of thinly peeled orange rind
3 large eggs
½ cup sugar
pinch of salt
1 teaspoon vanilla
¾ cup heavy cream
Sauce:
4 tablespoons butter
⅔ cup light brown sugar
pinch of salt
½ cup light cream
2-4 tablespoons bourbon or brandy

Cut each slice of bread into quarters and pack into a buttered baking dish, measuring about 9 inches square.

Combine the milk, cinnamon stick and orange rind in a saucepan and scald the milk. Remove from the heat, cover and leave to infuse for 20 minutes.

Lightly beat the eggs with the sugar, salt and vanilla in a mixing bowl. Strain in the milk and continue stirring until the sugar has dissolved. Pour the mixture over the bread and leave to soak for at least 45 minutes, pressing the bread down occasionally into the liquid.

Pour over the cream and soak 15 minutes longer.

Preheat the oven to 350°.

Place the baking dish in a roasting pan and pour hot water into the pan to come about 1 inch up the sides of the dish. Bake in this water bath for 35-45 minutes or until set and lightly browned on top.

Remove from the oven and leave to cool slightly while making the sauce.

Combine the butter, sugar and salt in a saucepan and heat, stirring to melt the butter and dissolve the sugar. Bring to a boil and boil 1 minute. Remove from the heat and cool slightly, then stir in the cream and bourbon.

Serve the bread pudding warm, cut into squares, with the hot sauce.

VARIATION: For a less rich sauce, combine 3 egg yolks and ⅓ cup sugar in a heatproof mixing bowl placed over a pan of hot water. Beat until the mixture is very pale and thick, then gradually beat in 3 tablespoons bourbon. Serve the sauce immediately as it will separate as it cools.

SERVES 6-8

CRÈME PRALINÉ

2 cups heavy cream
3 large egg yolks
¼ cup granulated sugar
1 teaspoon vanilla
¼ cup firmly packed light brown sugar
¼ cup finely chopped pecans

Preheat the oven to 300°.

Scald the cream. Beat the egg yolks with the granulated sugar and vanilla until the sugar has dissolved. Stir in the hot cream. Strain into six ramekins or other individual serving dishes.

Place the ramekins in a roasting pan and pour around hot water to come halfway up the sides of the ramekins. Bake in this water bath for 20-25 minutes or until just set. Remove from the water bath and cool.

Heat the broiler.

Mix together the brown sugar and pecans and sprinkle in an even layer over the top of the custards. Place under the broiler, about 5-6 inches from the source of heat, and cook gently until the topping has melted and caramelized. If the sugar begins to burn, move the ramekins further away from the heat. The caramelizing will take 4-5 minutes.

Cool and chill before serving.

SERVES 6

INDEX

All measurements in this book are given in American cups. These are available at major department stores. Imperial and metric conversions are given below:

DRY INGREDIENTS

Name US/UK	US Measure	UK equivalent
Bread crumbs	1 cup	50g/2oz
Cornmeal	1 cup	125g/4oz
Flour (all-purpose, self-rising/ plain, self-raising)	1 cup	125g/4oz
Graham Crackers/Digestive Biscuits	1 cup	150g/5oz
Masa Harina	½ cup	75g/3oz
Parmesan Cheese	1 cup	50g/2oz
Rice	1 cup	185g/6½oz
Sugar (confectioners'/icing)	1 cup	125g/4oz
Sugar (light or dark)	1 cup	175g/6oz
Sugar (granulated/caster or granulated)	½ cup	125g/4oz
Tortilla Chips	1 cup	50g/2oz

DAIRY PRODUCTS

Name US/UK	US measure	UK equivalent
Butter	1 stick	125g/4oz
	1 cup	225g/8oz
Cheese	1 cup	125g/4oz
Curd cottage cheese/curd cheese	1 cup	225g/8oz
Lard	1 cup	225g/8oz

FISH AND MEAT

Name US/UK	US measure	UK equivalent
Clams	1 cup	125g/4oz
Cooked meat	1 cup	150g/5oz
Crackling	½ cup	50g/2oz
Oysters (canned)	¾ cup	2 105g cans
Shrimp/Prawns	1 cup	125g/4oz

VEGETABLES

As a general rule, one cup of chopped vegetables weighs 125g/4oz. These are the exceptions:

Name US/UK	US measure	UK equivalent
Beans (all kinds)	1 cup	225g/8oz
Lettuce leaves	1 cup	4-6 leaves
Peas	1½ cups	225g/8oz
Pepper (fresh)	1 cup	1 pepper
Potato (mashed)	1 cup	225g/8oz
Potato (sweet)	¾ cup	200g/7oz

DRIED FRUIT/NUTS

Name US/UK	US measure	UK equivalent
Almonds, Hazelnuts, Pecans, Pine nuts, Walnuts	½ cup	50g/2oz
Coconut (desiccated and fresh, grated)	1 cup	100g/4oz
Figs (dried)	⅓ cup	50g/2oz
Raisins	½ cup	75g/3oz

FRUITS

Name US/UK	US measure	UK equivalent
Apples (sliced)	1 cup	125g/4oz
Bananas (sliced)	¾ cup	225g/8oz
Fruit Preserve	½ cup	150g/5oz
Grapes	1 cup	125g/4oz
Pineapple (canned)	1 cup	425g/15oz can
Pineapple (chopped)	1½ cups	½ medium pineapple

OVEN TEMPERATURES

	°F	°C	Gas Mark
Very cool	225	110	¼
	250	120	½
Cool	275	140	1
	300	150	2
Moderate	325	160	3
	350	180	4
Moderately hot	375	190	5
	400	200	6
Hot	425	220	7
	450	230	8
Very hot	475	240	9

LIQUIDS

US measure	UK equivalent
¼ cup	4 tablespoons
½ cup	120ml/4fl oz
1 cup	250ml/8 fl oz
2 cups	450ml/¾ pint

TERMS

US	UK
Apple pie spice	Mixed spice
Beet	Beetroot
Boneless sirloin steak	Rump steak
Canadian bacon	Smoked pork loin
Collard greens	Spring greens
Cornish game hens	Poussins
Cornstarch	Cornflour
Country sausage links	Pork sausages
Eggplant	Aubergine
Flank steak	Rump steak
Flounder	Plaice
Garbanzos	Chickpeas
Golden raisins	Sultanas
Ground round	Minced beef
Ground pork	Minced pork
Light corn syrup	Golden syrup
Monterey Jack cheese	Double Gloucester cheese
Navy beans	Haricot beans
Romaine lettuce	Cos lettuce
Round steak	Braising steak
Sausage	Sausagemeat
Scallions	Spring onions
Shoulder chop	Chump chop
Squabs	Small wood pigeons
Tenderloin	Fillet
Zucchini	Courgette